AMAZING PEOPLE FROM UKRAINE, AFGHANISTAN AND ACROSS OUR WORLD

REFUGEE HEROES

Published by:
Wilkinson Publishing Pty Ltd
ACN 006 042 173
Level 6, 174 Collins Street
Melbourne, VIC, Australia 3000
Ph: 03 9654 5446

enquiries@wilkinsonpublishing.com.au
www.wilkinsonpublishing.com.au

Title: Refugee Heroes: Amazing People from Ukraine, Afghanistan and Across Our World

ISBN: 9781922810144

eBook ISBN: 9781922810182

A catalogue record of this book is available from the National Library of Australia.

Design by Spike Creative Pty Ltd
Ph: (03) 9427 9500
spikecreative.com.au

Printed and bound in Australia by Griffin Press.

AMAZING PEOPLE FROM UKRAINE, AFGHANISTAN AND ACROSS OUR WORLD

REFUGEE HEROES

LAURIE NOWELL

CONTENTS

FOREWORD

Groucho Marx once famously described the art of politics as being about "looking for trouble, finding it everywhere, diagnosing it incorrectly, and applying the wrong remedies".

He probably wasn't talking about the politics surrounding refugees but in the current climate, Groucho Marx is looking pretty close to the mark. With Europe having opened its arms to refugees fleeing Ukraine, we meanwhile have cognitive dissonance in the UK and Denmark around keeping people out and sending asylum seekers to Africa. In numerous locations in Europe and across the Asia-Pacific, many Afghans are wondering what happened to the attention towards their country's plight and the promises of refugee places made amid the fall of Kabul in August 2021. Meanwhile, here in Australia, we have seen new political commitment to sending refugees far away and into the distant oblivion of offshore processing. On this, UNHCR's views are well known.

AMES was established in 1951, the same year in which the UN Refugee Convention came into being, a few years after the end of World War Two and, coincidentally, just a few months after the creation of UNHCR. In common at the time of our founding and enduring today, is a shared belief that the world can do better for refugees. That countries and communities are strongest when we work together. And that restoring a sense of agency and hope to someone who has fled persecution, conflict or war, is not only possible but demonstrably proven to be effective in building bonds, creating new foundations, restoring horizons and ultimately, making our communities and our world better.

AMES has been restoring horizons in Victoria and elsewhere in Australia, and across the world, ever since. And the stories in this book speak to just how life-changing this work can be. In its pages you will find unflinching accounts of the calamitous situations that led people to flee, reflections of the successes and failures of peace efforts, and perspectives on new lives and circumstances here in Australia that are being built through resilience and hope — a reminder that the best way for us all to understand and respond comes through listening to the refugees who have experienced this firsthand, as well as those in the community who work alongside them. It is their example that gives great cause for hope and optimism.

Adrian Edwards
Regional Representative for Australia, New Zealand and the Pacific
UNHCR, the UN Refugee Agency

INTRODUCTION

The pictures that came out of Russia's invasion of Ukraine in 2022 were chillingly similar to images of devastated cities from the Second World War.

The last major war in Europe established a world order that has lasted 70 years; it removed brutal autocratic dictators and established the supremacy of western liberal democracies. WWII also spawned the International Refugee Convention, which provides protection for people fleeing conflict or persecution.

There are now more than 100 million displaced people across the globe, the highest number in history. It is no accident that these numbers are currently so high as the world is again seeing regressive autocracies on the rise.

WWII was a watershed in the recognition and support for people deemed refugees. The conflict in Ukraine may also be a watershed. Just as many nations agreed to the International Refugee Convention in 1951, in 2018 more than 150 nations signed the Global Compact on Refugees, which seeks equitable responsibility-sharing for refugees and sustainable solutions to human displacement.

While the conflict in the Ukraine has galvanised the west in standing up to autocratic regimes, the question remains: will it give impetus to the search for lasting solutions to the global refugee crisis?

Europe's initial response to the Ukraine refugee crisis has been a commendably impressive show of solidarity in the face of a fast-moving emergency.

The Ukrainians, most of them women and children, have been welcomed, fed and housed in vast numbers.

But not unlike WWII, the scale of the crisis is staggering and coping with it into the future will require funds, commitment and international cooperation; and a plan will be needed to support Ukrainians to return to their homeland and rebuild it.

The support provided to Ukrainians raises the inevitable question about the international community's treatment of refugees from other countries.

To put that in perspective, in all of 2015 about a million Syrians, Afghans and Iraqis crossed the Mediterranean Sea to seek refuge in Europe, sparking talk of a "migration crisis". In the early part of the Ukraine conflict, about a million people a week left the country seeking safety. Some estimates say that as many as ten million Ukrainians will be forced to leave their homes as a result of the conflict.

Historian John Lukacs argued that the Allies' victory against autocracies in WWII bought the global community 50 years of relative stability and the opportunity to improve the lives people across it.

Lukacs claimed that standing up to autocratic and repressive regimes early in the piece was vital to the ultimate victory.

Among the fruits of this have been falling global poverty rates, the emancipation of women in many — though not all — parts of the world, improved educational opportunities in the developing world and new architecture in international law.

We have also seen the creation of the United Nations and its humanitarian agencies as a foil to the sometimes capricious and self-interested actions of nation states.

In recent times the United Nations has been an important actor and clearing house on the issue of climate change which, of itself, is already having an influence on migration and human displacement.

But the half century or so period of relative stability and economic and social progress we have enjoyed may be coming to an end.

A recent report by human rights NGO Freedom House says that global freedom is under siege with attacks on liberal democracy ramping up around the world.

The report found that autocracy is making gains against democracy and encouraging more leaders to abandon the democratic path to security and prosperity.

Countries which suffered democratic declines over the past year outnumbered those which strengthened democracy by more than two to one, it said.

The report concluded that the global order is nearing a tipping point, and if democracy's defenders do not work together to help guarantee freedom for all people, the authoritarian model could prevail.

With the world potentially on the brink of another period of worrying instability, perhaps global leaders should embrace the need for a coordinated and humane response to all of those fleeing war and other desperate circumstances.

This book tells the compelling stories of some of the people who have fled situations of conflict and violence that are largely the result of intransigent and brutal autocracies.

Refugees who settle in Australia bring with them memories, traditions, culture and history. They also bring with them hopes, dreams and ambitions for their children. They are, by definition, resilient and ingenious people who have overcome challenges and dangers just to get here.

These are the inspirational stories of ordinary people forced by circumstances beyond their control to make extraordinary physical and emotional journeys to safety and freedom.

CHAPTER 1
ESCAPING UKRAINE'S KILLING FIELDS

Anastasiia

Anastasiia Kozinaz, 33, fled Ukraine's killing fields for the sake of her two boys, leaving behind her husband, her family and everything she had known.

Anastasia's house was just a kilometre from Bucha and Irpin, the places just outside Kyiv where Russian troops are accused of massacring hundreds of civilians.

For two weeks the family sheltered in their basement as Russian shells and bombs rained down.

"It was terrible. All the time there were tanks, bombs and firing. All the time we were afraid the Russians would come. We spent nights in the basement and my sons became emotional. I had to talk to them about what they had seen," said Anastasiia.

Bucha was one of the first outlying areas of Kyiv that Russian forces occupied when they moved in on February 27, 2022. More than 300 people are said to have died in extra-judicial killings.

In neighbouring Irpin, more than a hundred are claimed to have been murdered.

Images of the killings emerged after Ukrainian forces reclaimed control of the whole Kyiv region and liberated towns from Russian troops.

Bodies with bound hands, close-range gunshot wounds and signs of torture lay scattered in the city after the Russians left.

Anastasiia and her two boys Maxim, 12, and Nikita, 10, escaped the carnage at the height of the fighting.

"My husband told me I must go for the sake of our boys. He said it was not clear whether our army would be able to stop the Russians," she said in broken English. "He stayed behind to look after my mother and our house."

The three made a dangerous 26-hour journey to Poland from where they flew to Australia on hastily organised tourist visas.

"A friend of my husband, who lives in Melbourne, told him to send us here. So here we are. I am glad that my sons are safe."

Using a translation service on her phone Anastasiia wrote words about how her whole world changed in an instant.

"On February 24, 2022, at about six o'clock in the morning, my husband called me. He was on a business trip to western Ukraine in Lviv," she wrote.

"Without explaining for a long time, he announced the shocking news and told me to go urgently to refuel the car. It took until noon, and it was then that I first saw and felt the missile hit the radar tower, which was near the gas station in the village of Svyatopetrivske.

"There was chaos and panic all around. I could not imagine what to do in such a situation. Tears rolled down my face all the time.

"My husband borrowed a car from friends and was already moving towards Kyiv. There were long queues at gas stations that were still working. In a few hours, due to many accidents, the road from Kyiv to Lviv turned into a traffic jam.

"At short intervals, at low altitudes, invading Russian planes flew by and bombed something. What everyone feared most and did not want to believe had begun — the war.

"At dawn, my husband drove home, handed over the borrowed car to his colleagues so that they could get home southwest of Kyiv, and gave his private car to his partner to get to his family in the northern suburbs of Kyiv at Brovary.

"For the next two weeks, due to continuous bombardment and shelling, we sat in the basement. During the day, my husband tried to find food, and at night, along with other neighbours, he was on duty with weapons at prepared positions.

"During these two weeks, my husband twice tried to send us to a safer region of the country, but when a significant part of the population tries to move from the north, east and south of the country to the west in such a short time, such movements become even more dangerous.

"After two weeks, we found the necessary gasoline and took a less safe route to Pochaiv, Ternopil region, to visit friends. It was at this time that the fiercest battles were fought for Stoyanka, Irpin, Bucha, and Gorenichi. The next settlement in line for the fight was ours — Shevchenkove (Bilogorodka), on the border of Kyiv.

"At this time, no more than a kilometre from our house, the bloodiest fighting happened along the Irpin River, and continuous round-the clock bombardment dominated the scene.

"You could hear no other noise and the blasts shattered the window glass and scattered rocket fragments on our house. I left Kyiv with the children. My husband remained.

"We are now in Melbourne and safe. Only now we are aware of the imminent danger that was on our doorstep and, unfortunately, came to the homes of residents of Stoyanka, Irpen, Bucha, Gostomel, and Borodyanka. Thousands of tortured and killed people are the result.

"I don't know how to make my children forget what war is! I don't know if I will find the strength to return to my home!"

Anastasiia said she was not sure what the future holds for her family and country.

"I don't know where all this ends. A lot of things have been destroyed — playgrounds and schools. There's a lot of burned equipment and corpses of people in the street."

But she said that her immediate priority was to make sure her sons were safe and well adjusted.

"They are lucky they did not see a lot of the destruction and the corpses. My husband and I tried not to panic so that our kids would not see it. I was studying psychology so I am trying to talk to the boys a lot about what has happened and to use relaxation methods for them.

"I think about the children and the consequences of what has happened. There is a risk they will suffer post-traumatic stress disorder (PTSD) in a year or two. But they need to develop and grow. They are now in an active phase of development and growth and that must be my focus.

"For now, we are safe here in Australia and my sons can get on with their lives in a peaceful situation."

Ulyana

Fellow Ukrainian refugee Ulyana Matsaienko has also found refuge in Australia after her home city of Kharkiv was attacked by the Russian army.

She woke up in the Kharkiv apartment she shared with her grandmother at 5am on February 24 to the sound of distant explosions.

"It was 5am on February 24 and I woke up hearing explosions. At first I thought it was fireworks. But when the windows started vibrating with the blasts, I realised it was not fireworks," Ulyana said.

"I heard the neighbour upstairs talking loudly as they were nervous. Then I called my mother and asked: 'Has it begun?' She said 'Yes'.

"Deep inside ourselves, we knew what was happening.

"For five days we slept in the basement. It was difficult to go out to buy food because of explosions and bombing. We lived in a district close to the countryside so it was closer to the fighting and there were many explosions hear our house.

"My mother and step-father's apartment became too dangerous, so they escaped to the countryside. And many people from my workplace moved to the west part of Ukraine because it is safer there," she said.

But Ulyana's father, who is a firefighter, has stayed in Kharkiv to fight the dozens of fires caused each day by shelling and incendiary bombs.

"My dad is a fireman and he goes to fires after the shelling and bombing. It's dangerous work and my dad wears a helmet and body armour. One of his colleagues, a 30-year-old man, died during the shelling recently, which makes me worry about my father a lot," she said.

Ulyana said that Russia's war crimes in Ukraine are unforgiveable.

"What the Russians have done in Bucha and other places is evil. It is unbelievable that this could happen in Europe in 2022.

"Ukrainians will never forget this. I am worried about mother and father-in-law who have moved to the countryside near Kharkiv. I'm worried that what happened in Bucha will happen where they are," she said.

Ulyana described how many Ukrainians have found refuge with relatives and friends across Europe and the globe.

"On the fifth day of the invasion I had the chance to escape. A niece of my grandmother in Germany helped some of my family to escape. We went to Poland and then to Germany. My godmother and her daughter went to London because they had friends living there. I had a cousin here in Melbourne and she said to me to come here. I had got a visa in Ukraine and so I was lucky to come here to Melbourne."

Ulyana says that for her and most Ukrainians the future remains unknowable but her immediate goal is to help her family still in her war-torn homeland.

"Even if we win the war, the economy will be broken for years. Many people have lost their jobs," she said. "I worked in the Dean's office at the National University of Railway Transport in Kharkiv; that was my career. I used to work and take guitar lessons and meet my friends but that has all gone now.

"I don't know when the conflict will end. Maybe when the president of Russia is dead. But for me, now my plan is to stay here and find job so I can help my family," she said.

Ulyana took some dramatic photos showing bomb and missile explosions as well as the damage to buildings in her neighbourhood.

"It was unreal, like a scene from a movie. Everyone was shocked that these things were happening among us," she said.

CHAPTER 2
AFGHAN FAMILY'S DOUBLE 'MIRACLE'

For Afghan refugee Atefa Ibrahimi, arriving in Australia has been a double miracle.

The first piece of fortune was being able to get her family into Kabul's airport to escape the brutal clutches of the Taliban. The second was life-saving brain surgery that her father underwent just days after arriving in Melbourne.

Atefa's father Khan Ali had been sick since 2019 suffering headaches, low sodium levels and disorientation.

But his condition was not diagnosed until he arrived in Australia after being evacuated from Kabul along with thousands of others fleeing the Taliban.

He had a tumour on his pituitary gland which would have ultimately killed him but it was removed by brain surgeons at Melbourne's Cabrini Hospital. Khan Ali is recovering after spending 35 days in hospital.

Atefa, who worked in public affairs at the Australian embassy in Kabul, shared her family's remarkable story in the hope that it would raise awareness about the impact the Taliban's return is having on the majority of Afghanistan's population.

"My father had been sick since 2019 but when we came to Australia we got a diagnosis for the first time," Atefa said.

"It was a tumour on his pituitary gland. It's been a really difficult time for us with a lot of things going on and having to take care of our family. We were happy to at least get a diagnosis and see Dad get really good care. If we had stayed in Afghanistan, he would not have received the care and treatment he has," she said.

Atefa and her family arrived in Australia on September 5 and entered hotel quarantine in Darwin. Ten days later her father's health began to deteriorate.

When they arrived in Melbourne on September 19, Khan Ali was almost unconscious. Two days later he was rushed to hospital in an ambulance.

"I called my case manager and the nurses arranged an ambulance to take him away. It was very difficult for us culturally. In Afghanistan we would have travelled with him but because of COVID we couldn't," Atefa said.

"But we trusted the health system here and the doctors and nurses have been very kind to my dad."

As she speaks, Atefa and her sister Rabia pour tea from an ornate old silver teapot given to them by a volunteer mentor shortly after they arrived in Australia.

"Serving tea and offering hospitality is important to Afghans so we wanted to get a nice teapot and our mentor found us one," Atefa said.

Atefa and her family moved from their home in Wardak Province in 2001 because of the worsening security situation and to find refuge from nomadic groups who harassed and attacked them and their village annually.

"We moved to Kabul and we had normal lives. I was working with different national and international organisations, including the Australian embassy," Atefa said.

But that all changed in August this year when the Taliban took control of Kabul.

As the Taliban became masters of the beleaguered nation on August 15, Atefa and her family navigated their way through a series of militant checkpoints and made it to Kabul's international airport.

There, they saw suicide bombing attacks, tear gas and human stampedes but eventually made it into the safety of the airport terminal.

Atefa says the family were in danger because of her work and her activism in human rights movements, and particularly women's rights.

"Lots of people knew me because I was managing small, grassroots projects across the country. I also ran a library which was very popular in poor communities where minority groups such as Hazara and Shia lived," she said.

Her mixed ethnicity also made her family a potential target for the Sunni-dominated Taliban.

"I have merged ancestry with a Hazara mother, a Qizilbash father and a Pashtun grandmother. That put our family at risk, particularly because of the Hazara and Shia connection," Atefa said.

The family made three separate attempts to get into the airport on three separate days.

"Getting into the airport was a miracle. The first time we tried there was gunfire and confusion. It was hopeless and a risky time for us," Atefa said.

"The second time we spent a whole night at the gate we were told to go to but it did not open. We didn't see any hope at that point and we went home because we had a newborn baby with us and my father was ill," she said.

Atefa then waited for instructions from the embassy that would be their last chance to reach safety.

"We waited all night for a message but there was nothing and we felt in danger. Eventually, the next day, we went back to the airport," she said.

"We had to go through checkpoints. At one point a Taliban militant pointed a gun muzzle at my kidneys and said 'get lost or I'll kill you'. Even though I was disguised, he knew I was a woman when he said this. He seemed to be kind because I was helping my elderly dad."

At 11pm Atefa was able to contact some American friends who guided the family to a gate at the airport that would accept them.

Atefa and her brother plunged into a sewerage drain to be able to get to the gate.

She had taken with her a prized Australian embassy notebook which she hoped would act as a sign to help her get through airport checkpoints.

"My ID card was so small it was hard for people to see, so I took along my notebook. We also had an umbrella as a kind of code — but none of this worked.

"We also called out a pre-arranged code word for a long time but nothing happened," she said.

Eventually, Atefa called her American friend who spoke to the soldiers on the gate and got the family inside.

"It was a miracle. We were really lucky. My brother went back for the rest of the family and, in all, 14 of us made it into the airport and we were transferred to the Australian camp inside the airport.

"Our ordeal lasted almost a week. I was very worried about my Dad who was very ill. I didn't want to take him on the journey but I had no choice. We feared that people left behind would be taken by the Taliban," Atefa said.

Atefa and her family were among around 130,000 people airlifted out of Kabul by US, UK, Australian and other nations' military aircraft between August 14 and 25, 2021.

Since the Taliban's takeover in Afghanistan, a humanitarian crisis has beset the country.

Conflict and insecurity, drought, COVID-19 and an economy in freefall are driving increased levels of poverty and pushing Afghanistan to the brink of collapse, according to the United Nations.

Five and a half million people are internally displaced — roughly the population of Finland — including more than 670,000 forced to leave their homes so far this year, 60 per cent of whom are children.

And what started as a drought crisis has spiralled into economic disaster, with nine in 10 major urban centres also expected to face extreme hardship, as debts pile up and savings dwindle.

The already widespread drought looks set to worsen, as farmers and herders endure a second consecutive year of drought in 2022, with La Niña bringing drier than normal conditions across Afghanistan.

The increasing numbers of people returning to the country over recent years has compounded the challenges.

More than a million Afghans have returned from Iran and Pakistan since 2018, while others are trying to leave the country.

Climate change has also had an impact in Afghanistan, contributing to internal displacement. The UN estimates that around 70 per cent of the population has been impacted by drought and flooding and crop failures.

Atefa's notebook

Using her Australian embassy notebook, Atefa has recorded some of her thoughts during her traumatic journey from Afghanistan to Australia.

She titled the first page in Persian language as *"Notes of a girl who might become a refugee..."*

On August 14 she wrote:

> *Today I decided I must leave Afghanistan and that is the most difficult decision I am making. Spoke with friends to help me prepare a letter to help me get out.*
>
> *We may go with family or without family; or we may die.*
>
> *You live or you die; how traumatic it is. The Taliban is here bringing insecurity. How did we get to this point?*

Days later she wrote:

> *Finally I became a refugee. We are still travelling. But not at home yet? Now I am in the Australian camp at Dubai.*

CHAPTER 3

REFUGEES' EPIC JOURNEYS TO FREEDOM ACROSS THE "ROOF OF THE WORLD"

Tibetan refugees Palden and Tashi Tensing made perilous month-long treks over the highest mountains in the world to find new lives in peace and safety.

On their separate journeys, they dodged trigger-happy Chinese soldiers, survived raging torrents and nights lost in dense forests; and they walked for days blinded by blizzards and half frozen by snowdrifts.

Ultimately, they found sanctuary from the invaders who had enslaved their country — and they found each other.

Palden says that for him life in Tibet became increasingly untenable as the Chinese Communist Party, which annexed his country in 1949, increased its control on daily life and effectively banned Buddhism and the Tibetan language.

Thousands of Tibetans have been jailed for having a photo of Tibet's spiritual leader His Holiness the Dalai Lama and for teaching Buddhist beliefs.

Palden said that as he approached adulthood Tibetans could not access higher education or well-paid jobs.

"It was very difficult in Tibet. The Chinese discriminated against Tibetans and considered us barbarians," Palden said.

"I was not happy with this. I could not talk freely about politics or the Tibetan nation. There were no educational opportunities and if you didn't learn Chinese, you had no career."

So, in 1998, aged 18, he left Tibet and followed the pathway of the Dalai Lama and 80,000 other Tibetans who fled Chinese oppression and trekked over the Himalayas in 1959 to found a Tibetan community and government-in-exile at Dharamshala, in India.

"I walked 29 days over the Himalayas into Nepal. It was dangerous because the Chinese soldiers would have shot us if that had seen us. We were in a group of 12 and we travelled in autumn so it was very cold. We had to sleep out in the open so we took with us warm clothes," he said.

To eat on the strenuous journey, the group took along balls of Tsamba, a Himalayan staple made of glutinous barley flour meal mixed with the salty Tibetan butter tea.

There was a tense moment when the escapees approached the Tibet-Nepal border at 1am.

"We saw the Chinese trucks blocking the road as we approached the border, and their tents were everywhere. I saw a soldier on the truck and carrying a gun lifted to his shoulder. We got off the road and got into a river that ran beside the road. We crept past the Chinese and got away. If the soldiers had seen us, they would have shot us," he said.

Tashi's journey, six years earlier when she was aged just five, was just as perilous.

She set out with her brother, two monks, a women and a friend as a guide. Her father had passed away and her mother sent her children to India for a better life.

"The journey was very difficult. We walked at night because it was safer," Tashi said.

"There was lots of snow and as we crossed over the top of the Himalayan range there was a blizzard and we couldn't see the road. We waited two hours for the weather to clear but we lost the road because our eyes were blinded by the snow. Eventually, the storm stopped and we found the way."

As way of giving thanks, Tashi and her companions placed stones on the road as sign to others following behind — a tradition now for Tibetans fleeing to India.

Before reaching safety, Tashi became lost alone in a dense forest one dark night.

"We walked separated in the dark for safety and one night I lost the road and become lost in a forest all night," she said. "My brother and our guide came to look for me and eventually found me. It was a scary time."

Her travelling companions separated into small groups to cross the border into Nepal but the two monks were arrested by police.

"They were sent back to the Chinese police and were beaten and put in jail," Tashi said.

She and her remaining group made their way to the Tibetan Government's reception centre in Kathmandu and were processed by the UNHCR. They then caught a bus to Dharamshala.

Both Tashi and Palden worked for the Tibetan government in India. They met at a Tibetan college in 2002 and married in India.

Palden says the couple were happy in India at first. He worked designing curricula for Tibetan language studies and Tashi for the Tibetan government's health service.

"We were free and the Indian people were very kind to Tibetans but financially it was very difficult and documentation became more of a problem," he said.

In 2018, Palden went to the US to speak at a conference on the Tibetan language.

On his return, he was interviewed by Indian authorities because he had no passport.

"I was not allowed to enter India and the Indian immigration authorities looked into my case for three hours because I didn't have a passport. Tibetans cannot get passports in India. We have permits that need to be renewed each year." Palden said.

Documentation continued to be an issue for Palden in India when he was repeatedly accused by police of being a "foreigner" amid growing Hindu nationalism across the country.

And both Palden and Tashi began to harbour fears for their young daughter Tensing Dickey as gender abuse and rape became more prevalent across India.

Their application to come to Australia as refugees was granted and they arrived in 2019 just before the COVID-19 pandemic struck.

Locked down in a small flat with two young children in Melbourne's inner west, the family turned to their spiritual leader for advice and solace.

The Dalai Lama has been talking remotely, using technology, to connect with thousands of Tibetans across the globe.

"His holiness has been talking about positive emotions, positive thinking to help people get through the pandemic to give people peace of mind in a difficult time," Palden said. "We have also been teaching our daughter Tibetan during this time."

Palden and Tashi are now building a new life in Melbourne with support from migrant and refugee settlement agency AMES Australia through the Australian Government's Humanitarian Settlement Program.

The couple and their two children are on now pathways to establishing themselves. Through the HSP they have been provided with services including essential registrations, housing, orientation and links to health and education services.

Palden and Tashi are keen to find work and build new lives. Having improved their English, the couple have identified training opportunities and enrolled in courses.

Tashi is currently studying childcare and hopes to eventually find work. Palden has also begun studying to be an operating theatre technician.

The couple say they are happy and grateful to be in Australia.

"We love life in Australia and the opportunities that our children have here. We are determined to find work and support ourselves and enjoy all that Australia has to offer," Tashi said.

Tibet came under Chinese control in October 1951 after failed attempts by the Tibetan government to gain international recognition.

In 1959, after a failed anti-Chinese uprising, the 14th Dalai Lama fled Tibet and set up a government in exile in India.

Most of Tibet's monasteries were destroyed in the 1960s and 1970s during China's Cultural Revolution and thousands of Tibetans are believed to have been killed during periods of repression and martial law.

The Dalai Lama has claimed 1.2 million people have been killed under Chinese rule and that China has actively suppressed the Tibetan identity.

CHAPTER 4
UKRAINIAN SISTERS' FLIGHT TO FREEDOM

Two Ukrainian sisters have found refuge in Australia after braving bombs and snipers in a desperate journey to safety.

Yevheniia Cherkasova, 24, and her sister Alexandra, 14, fled besieged Kharkiv as Russian tanks attempted to encircle the city.

After surviving bombing and missile strikes, the sisters were put aboard a train by their parents in the precarious hope they would reach safety.

Now safe in Melbourne, they have told of the human, economic and emotional toll the Russian invasion has taken on themselves and their beleaguered nation.

As the Russian attack on Kharkiv began, Yevheniia's immediate emotion was disbelief.

At home with her family in their comfortable apartment close to the centre of the city, she struggled to process the idea that her world was about to be turned upside down. Just a few weeks later it was equally difficult to comprehend that she was headed for the other side of the world.

"I thought maybe it was fireworks but far away. But then they started to bomb the city centre and we knew what it was. It was the Russians attacking us," Yevheniia said.

"At 5am in the morning and we all woke up. We heard loud noises from the street. There were explosions not far from us — maybe 10 kilometres away.

"At first we didn't think it was war but then there was a factory explosion and when we read the news we realised it was war.

"We all went to the window in the kitchen and saw a mushroom cloud and the sky was much brighter than it should have been at that time in the morning. It was then that it really sank in what was happening," she said.

As the Russian attack continued, Yevheniia and her parents went to check on the craft shop they own and run.

"It is small shop but I loved working there because I do a lot of craft. We sold yarn, beads for embroidery and material for crochet," she said.

"We had a lot of customers from other countries, so it helped my English a lot. I learned English at school but we would have lots of foreign students come to the shop. We got to the shop at 8am. It is five kilometres from the border of the city, on a ring road, and less than 40 kilometres from the Russian border.

"Then we tried to reach my grandparents who live in a small village closer to the border. But the Russians were occupying this village. For the first two weeks we heard nothing from them. Even now my parents can't call them, but my grandparents can call them when there is a connection. My grandparents are trapped with no electricity or gas. They are surviving by cooking soup on an open fire."

A couple of weeks into the conflict, Yevheniia and her family also suffered blackouts.

"We had some days in Kharkiv where there was no electricity or water. It was scary because we had no electricity or internet connections, no water and we didn't know what was happening because we couldn't see or read the news," she said.

Yevheniia's parents sent her and her sister away on March 13 after a missile hit houses across the street from their apartment.

"Our parents put us in the car and drove us to the railway station. They put us on a train to Lviv in the west of Ukraine and then we made it into Poland," she said.

"At the time, we were lucky because there were not so many people. We got the first train to the border. It was not scheduled, so it was not so crowded and we could sit down. But I have friends who spent 26 hours on their feet, trying to get out of the country by train."

Yevheniia says it was eerie and frightening travelling across the recently peaceful but now devastated countryside.

"It was scary looking out of the train travelling across the country. We went through Kiev and other places that had been bombarded. We could see bombed buildings and wrecked cars. Ordinary people had obviously been killed by the Russians. I remembered how these places were supposed to look and now all I could see was ruins. My city Kharkiv is Ukraine's second largest. It has beautiful old buildings, lots of industry and factories and universities. It was heart-breaking to see it under attack," Yevheniia said.

The Russian army attacked the northern suburbs of Kharkiv on February 25 after a massive artillery barrage.

Ukrainian forces were able to hold out against the Russian forces but bitter fighting continued for weeks on the outskirts of the city.

And incessant shelling killed dozens of civilians, including children.

It took the sisters two days to reach the Polish border. Again, they were lucky to be able to cross the border in just a few hours. Other refugees spent 16 hours or more getting though border posts.

They arrived in the Polish town of Bialystok, where champion junior speed skater Alexandra's ream had been based for training.

"We were able to stay with the team for a while but it was hard in Poland. It was difficult to find a job and we had no money or extra clothes," Yevheniia said.

"We were faced with having to pay for accommodation and food in Poland with no job and little money."

It was then that Maxim, a family friend who has lived in Australia for a decade, reached out to the sisters.

"Our friend told us about the Australian program to offer tourist visas to Ukrainians and we and we applied," Yevheniia said.

"After we got our visas we flew 27 hours through Warsaw and Istanbul to Melbourne. Melbourne is a beautiful city and very peaceful. We were very scared and so we are happy and grateful to be here."

Yevheniia said other family members had found refuge in other parts of Europe but her parents were still in Ukraine.

She said that a sad outcome of the conflict in Ukraine was that it had split families with links to Russia.

"My father has a brother living in Russia and he told my Dad that Russia was only attacking military targets. They had a huge fight over that and have fallen out. Most Ukrainian families who have connections in Russia have had arguments about what is happening. People inside Russia have been fooled by propaganda. They are not hearing about civilians being killed and people losing their houses."

Yevheniia says every family in Ukraine knows someone who has lost everything.

"In my grandparents' village, a lot of people were robbed by the Russians. They raided a beauty salon there and took everything — mirrors, blow dryers and even chairs. Why do they need chairs? They don't have chairs in Russia?"

Yevheniia said that even Ukrainians who were once in favour of closer ties with Russia have now changed their minds.

"Ukraine was a bit divided over our relationship with Russia — we do have historic, cultural and family ties — but no one wants to be close to Russia now," she said.

Yevheniia said that Ukrainian President Volodymyr Zelenskyy has reunited Ukraine in the face of Russian aggression.

"Since becoming independent, Ukraine has not really been united until now. At first no one thought Zelenskyy would be such a strong leader," she said.

"People thought he was very young — in his 40s — when most world leaders are much older. But whatever happens from now, Zelenskyy will be remembered as a great leader."

Asked what she would say to Russian President Vladimir Putin given the chance, Yevheniia said, "I would say just — why? In 2014 when Russia attacked the eastern part of Ukraine and Crimea, it seemed like he had a plan — an evil plan — but a plan. Now there doesn't seem to be a plan and it is not going to end well for Putin."

Yevheniia says she is uncertain about the future and where how the conflict in her homeland will end up.

"I didn't think it would be so bad. And I never understood how much I loved my country until this whole thing happened. When the war started we thought it would be over in a few weeks. And then we thought it would be just one week more, one week more... But it hasn't stopped yet and we are just hoping for the best every day.

"I don't know what the future holds but I hope the war ends soon and we can go home and rebuild our country. About 1200 houses have been destroyed in Kharkiv — that's a lot of people. We will rebuild but things will never be the same after this."

CHAPTER 5

MINISTER'S PHONE CALL PUT AFGHAN FAMILY ON FLIGHT TO SAFETY

When prominent Afghan journalist Khalid Amiri was desperately trying to find a way into Kabul's international airport to secure his family's escape from the Taliban, salvation came from 11,000 kilometres away.

His saviour was then Australian federal minister Senator Linda Reynolds. She played a personal role in getting Khalid's family out of Afghanistan during the dramatic airlift evacuation in August 2021.

Khalid said the Senator was asked by a mutual Afghan friend, who was senior official in the Afghan government, to help him and his family to escape the Taliban.

She agreed to help and was in close contact with Khalid during the harrowing days as he attempted to get into Kabul's Hamid Karzai airport.

At one point, Senator Reynolds even spoke to a US marine through Khalid's phone at an airport gate to request that he look after Khalid and his family until Australian officials could ensure that the Amiri's departure went smoothly.

The senator explained to the marine that Khalid and his family had Australian visas and the soldier showed great kindness in helping Khalid and his parents and four sisters get to the Australian pick up point near the Baron Hotel.

"We are happy and grateful to have received such a warm welcome from the Australian Government and people. My mum says Senator Reynolds is an angel sent from God for us," Khalid said.

Senator Reynolds' help was just one episode in Khali's family's incredible journey to safety.

Now resettled in Melbourne with his parents and four sisters, Khalid says his connection with Senator Reynolds was the difference between making it to safety and becoming a potential target of the Taliban.

"I was in contact with Senator Reynold through WhatsApp and I sent her a text to say they were not accepting my visa," Khalid said. "She phoned me and asked to speak to the US marine. She spoke to him for a minute and then he let us through and we were taken to the Australian army base."

Khalid was forced to flee his career in digital media with the national broadcaster RTA (Radio Television Afghanistan) where he was a senior producer and presenter.

"It was hard to leave a job I was passionate about. I was working 12 to 15 hours a day for something I believed in and thinking that our democracy and national government was getting stronger. One day I was writing about how the national army was getting stronger and repulsing the Taliban and next I was writing news that the Taliban are entering Kabul.

"We were shattered and broken-hearted at the channel. As state TV station employees we had been publishing anti-Taliban propaganda, so everyone was worried. I felt I had to stay on but some of the younger staff members said they wanted to go home so I told them to go and be safe.

"We had already been getting threatening messages from the Taliban saying that we should be calling their dead fighters 'martyrs' in our reports. When we refused, they would say things like 'get ready we are going to blow up you and your TV station'."

He said there was general panic when people realized the Taliban were taking control of the capital.

"Everyone rushed home that afternoon. I packed my laptop in my bag and went home. I was told to switch off my phone because I could be tracked by its signal," Khalid said.

"My mum was crying when I got home. She was saying 'they will look for you'. So I moved in with a relative who lived in another part of Kabul. I was there for four or five days and then I went to the airport."

Helped by an actor friend, Khalid used some theatre craft and subterfuge (the details of which he does not want to reveal) to get past several Taliban checkpoints and reach Kabul's international airport.

There, he was reunited with his parents and four sisters who had made their way there separately. However, their troubles were only just beginning.

Khalid and his family spent two nights outdoors at the airport trying to find a way in and on to a plane.

"It was very difficult and scary. A lot of my friends didn't make it to the airport and there were people climbing over each other," he said.

"There was tear gas and heavy gunfire into the air. My mum fainted twice and my baby sister was frightened. There was no food but we were able to buy bottles of water from some boys."

After a night out in the open Khalid manoeuvred his family close to one of the entries across a half-meter deep sewerage drain. On the other side of the gap were US soldiers.

"I got into the drain to try to get the coalition soldiers to see my visas — I was there from 11pm to 6am. The soldiers started asking for nationals — for US and British passport holders and others," he said.

"I tried to show them my visas which were printed out but they said they could not accept paper documents."

It was then that Khalid's contact with Minister Reynolds paid off.

"I was in contact with Ms Reynold through WhatsApp and I sent her a text to say they were not accepting my visa. She phoned me and asked to speak to the soldier. She spoke to him for a minute and then he let us through and were taken to the Australian army base. The moment we were safe we breathed a sigh of relief that we were in safe hands. We were on open ground with other families and their bags from 11am till about 3am when we got on a military flight which took us to Dubai where we spent eight days in a camp on a US airbase," he said.

Khalid said he felt relieved to be safe but guilty at having left so many friends and colleagues behind.

"I was feeling like I had betrayed the people I had left behind and my country. It was strange feeling because the last time I had been through that airport, I was wearing a suit. Now all I had was a bag with my laptop a spare pair of jeans and an extra T-shirt."

From Dubai, Khalid and his family were flown to Darwin, where they went into COVID-19 quarantine, and then to Melbourne.

Khalid says that while in Dubai, he struck up a conversation with an Australian soldier.

"He asked me what I was reading. I said I didn't have anything to read but that I was keen to get hold of a book called *The Subtle Art of Not Giving a F#$%* which is about how to live a good and happy life when things do not always go well. He returned a few days later with a copy of the book he had written in it: 'Welcome to Australia. You are just as much as Aussie as the rest of us'. I will always treasure that book."

He says that despite the trauma of fleeing his homeland is optimistic about his future.

"I am happy and grateful to have received such a warm welcome from the Australian Government and people. But I don't want to be called a refugee forever. I want to develop a career in the media here in Australia," he said.

Since arriving in Melbourne, Khalid says he is still processing what happened in Afghanistan.

"I'm still in trauma. Every morning I wake up and think it's a dream. But then I realised it isn't and that this is my new reality. What hurts most is that we never deserved this. The international community, world leaders and our own president betrayed us. All the progress made on women's rights, girls education and ethnic minority rights vanished in one night. It's like the world has thrown us to the wolves. Leaving one's home, leaving one's country is hard. There's a saying in Afghanistan that no one puts their children in a boat unless they feel it is safer than the land. So being a refugee is a hard thing. The world needs to remember that every refugee once had a wonderful life back home, they had a good job and wonderful living — but all this was snatched from us."

He said that the Taliban could not be trusted to live up to promises that they would be inclusive.

"An example is how the Taliban have banned girls from schools and they have disbanded the ministry for women from the cabinet. It doesn't seem an inclusive government. There has been the exclusion of important ethnic and religious groups. The Taliban has zero tolerance of other ethnic groups; they believe in hijacking absolute power.

"What has happened in Afghanistan sends a message to young people in Afghanistan. What it says is that even though you have studied for years and gone to university, you are to be deprived of your rights and your jobs. There's a very dark picture ahead for the Afghan people."

Khalid said that he left Afghanistan with almost nothing.

"I had with me a bag on my shoulder with my laptop containing my work and data and memories. And with a single pair of spare jeans and an extra T-shirt I had to leave my life behind. It is heartbreaking to leave behind the things you have worked for and the things you dreamed of doing. It's hard to become a refugee; and no one becomes a refugee unless their home is taken away from them.

"Giving up your whole life, your relatives, family and friends and setting up in a new corner of the world with new hopes and a new pathway is very challenging and traumatic.

"Right now, I'm still passing through anxiety not knowing what future awaits me. But still, I'm happy I made it here to Australia with mum and my sisters — but I still have my elder brother and sister in Afghanistan which causes us worry. We'll do our best to get them out.

"But it's not only my family, there are hundreds and thousands of people across Afghanistan who want to get out. And not just people who worked with the coalition or western embassies.

"There are young, bright people — sportspeople, cricketers, singers, artists, poets — who believe that there's now no future for them under the Taliban.

"The international community needs to hear their voices and do something for them because leaving them behind would be a big betrayal."

His ambition was to build a media career here in Australia. He is now studying a Master's Degree in International Relations at Melbourne University.

"Journalism is my passion and I studied it at university. Back in Afghanistan I had a career working for a TV station representing my people and talking about issues. I would love to continue that work," Khalid said.

CHAPTER 6
SYRIAN CAFÉ PROVIDING FOOD FOR THE SOUL

In a quiet laneway in the Melbourne suburb of St Kilda there is a slice of Syria.

The Flavours of Syria Café has been established by asylum seeker chef Nayran Tabiei, who fled both Iran and Syria as a refugee from brutal, authoritarian regimes.

Nayran, her husband Majid, a qualified IT engineer, and daughter Alnour were detained on Christmas Island before settling in Melbourne.

Until recently Nayran ran a catering business under her Flavours of Syria banner, cooked meals for the needy, and hosted popular cooking classes with social enterprise Free to Feed, which offers food-related business opportunities to refugees.

With the help of Space2B, an art and design social enterprise that supports migrants and refugees, Nayran established the café to bring authentic Syrian food to Melburnians.

Each morning she makes the hour-long drive from her home to the café, a small indoor-outdoor space in the laneway behind trendy Chapel Street.

"I feel like I'm flying here in the mornings; like I'm going to my grandma's house. And I have tried to recreate my grandma's kitchen here," Nayran said.

She and Majid have decorated the café in middle-eastern style, with blue Syrian tiles, rugs and soft furnishings. In the corner are wreaths of garlic and onions — a tradition in most Syrian kitchens.

"We want people to feel like they're in Syria. It's been a long-time dream of mine to share something of my culture with people — to see smiling faces eating and drinking," Nayran said.

"They come and they feel like they're in Syria and I feel like I'm back in Syria in my grandma's house. I'm just doing what my grandma told me to do — to put my soul into everything I do and our customers feel that – even people who don't know us."

In keeping with her philosophy of giving back, Nayran is giving training and work experience opportunities to other refuges and asylum seekers. She also provides cooking classes and catering services.

"We want to give people the opportunity to start their own businesses so we are teaching them how to make coffee, cooking and hospitality. I'm taking my food to the wider community. Australian people have been so welcoming to us. I feel blessed to be here and so I'm happy to cook and serve," she said.

Dishes include stuffed eggplant and a light chicken and sumac wrap called mesakhan, baba ghanoush and hummus.

Nayran and Majid are refugees twice over.

In 2010, for the second time in their lives, the couple were forced to flee their home, leaving behind their possessions, friends, and established lives when the Damascus café they operated was collateral damage in bombing by Sunni rebels opposed to the brutal regime of Syrian President Bashar al Assed.

A few years earlier they had owned a successful wedding catering and clothing business in Tehran, Majid's home city.

But when local religious authorities objected to them allowing brides and grooms to meet under the same roof to decide on wedding arrangements, they were subject to a Sharia law 'haram' and banned from operating their business.

What's more, the religious authorities seized their building and turned them into social and legal outcasts, forcing them to leave Iran for Syria.

The couple moved from to Nayran's hometown Damascus in 2010

where they opened their restaurant.

"I lost my belongings, my life, two times," Majid said, speaking from his home in Melbourne's western suburbs. "It was terrible. We were living in an area of Damascus which the rebels were targeting. People were being killed and everything was destroyed."

Majid and Nayran sent their three sons to live with Majid's mother in Tehran to avoid the conflict but kept their young daughter Alnour with them as they searched for a new place to settle down somewhere in the Middle East.

They tried Tajikistan, Turkey, Afghanistan, and even Bali but could not find anywhere safe that would accept them.

They applied for asylum in the US three times but were refused. The difficulty of their search for a new home was compounded because as an Iranian, every time he wanted to travel to another country Majid had to return to Iran.

"We could not return to Syria because of the fighting and if I went back to Iran I might end up in prison," Majid said.

It was while the family was in Indonesia investigating the prospect of setting up a business there that they heard about the possibility of getting on a boat to Australia.

As refugees from Syria, they had registered themselves with the UN in Jakarta as asylum seekers but were told they faced a wait of three years before their claim could be processed.

Majid said it was a difficult decision to get on a small and possibly unseaworthy boat but at the time they were faced with few alternatives.

"When we arrived in Jakarta the taxi drivers were asking us if we wanted to go to Australia. I wasn't sure what they meant but it turned out they were not taxi drivers but people smugglers. They said to us 'why wait three years, give me money and I'll take you by boat'. We didn't trust them at first and thought they might just rob us but then we met people who had relatives taken to Australia by the smugglers. So we decided to go," he said

Majid said the three-day journey with 63 other people on a small fishing boat was hellish.

"It was a terrible journey — all the time I was vomiting. I spent three days beside the exhaust pipe breathing in fumes. But we were lucky. I heard stories of other boats that took much longer and had 200 people aboard. And of course some even sank."

The family reached Christmas Island in 2012 where they spent four months in detention before being transferred to another centre at Port Augusta, in South Australia, eventually settling in Melbourne.

They were released into the community in Melbourne at Easter in 2013 and were granted work rights in June 2016.

Nayran is also worried about her three sons — now in their 20s — living with Majid's mother in Iran.

"I am afraid for them and I want to bring them to be with me here, so they are safe," she said.

Alnour, now 15, considers herself Australian. She speaks English with an Aussie accent and is excelling in school.

CHAPTER 7
SISTERS REUNITED AFTER EPIC JOURNEYS TO SAFETY

Two sisters who fled the brutal military regime in Eritrea — each following a different but equally tortuous pathway to freedom and safety — are now rebuilding their lives in Australia.

Allae and sister Yara braved brutal beatings, people smuggler gangs, desperate night-time border crossings as well as the capricious nature of African continental politics in their epic quests for a new life free of fear and oppression.

And the sisters both have first-hand knowledge of the brutal and authoritarian regime of self-proclaimed Eritrean President Isaias Afewerki.

For two decades, President Afewerki has ruled Eritrea with an iron fist. Human rights groups say forced conscription of young people into military service has been prolonged indefinitely despite a decree limiting it to 18 months.

Political opponents are often jailed indefinitely without trial. Independent media is prohibited, and journalists imprisoned. Political parties and non-governmental organisations are also prohibited; elections, a legislature, and an independent judiciary have all been abolished because the President argues they would weaken Eritrea's defences.

In addition, some religious groups are forbidden altogether while others are strictly regulated by the government.

After years of struggle, Allae and Yara, whose names have been changed to protect family members still in Eritrea, are now living and studying in Melbourne's northern suburbs.

Despite the COVID-19 outbreak and its attendant lockdowns, they are happy and grateful to be where they are.

But life might have turned out very differently for them.

Allae left Eritrea in 2016 as the oppressive regime in her homeland tightened its omnipotent control over her life and her "difficult situation" became more desperate.

"Eritrea is ruled by a dictator and there is military law. As high school students, we couldn't graduate unless we completed Year 12 at a military education camp called SAWA, 300 kilometres from our hometown of Keren," Allae said.

"We had heard a lot of bad stuff about the place. There were terrifying stories about how students were treated. The military were abusing students in what was a kind of slavery."

In August 2019 the NGO Human Rights Watch (HRW) reported that students were fleeing Eritrea to avoid training at the SAWA camp, where they are subjected to systematic abuse, torture, harsh working conditions and punishments.

"Eritreans are subject to arbitrary arrest and harsh treatment in detention. Eritrea has had no national elections, no legislature, no independent media and no independent non-governmental organisations since 2001. Religious freedom remains severely curtailed," HRW said.

Allae said she and her parents were afraid of the prospect of military service but we had no option.

"In July 2014, I had to go there. It was a terrible time. We were woken up at 2am every morning. We were forced to clean the entire camp till 6am. We were given a small slice of bread and tea for breakfast and then we went to classes. But there really wasn't any education. After classes we were sent to work on farms owned by the military officers running the camp.

"Every Sunday we would walk for three hours on foot to reach a place called Molover, a big Agro-industry farm, and all farming activities were done by us. We spent about five hours working non-stop there. And then we would walk back to our camp for another three hours. We were not allowed to take a rest throughout. It was very hard work and there was a lot of abuse. One day I was sick and I asked if I could rest. The officer didn't allow me to rest. But because I was ill, I couldn't do a lot of work. The officer thought I was slacking, and he beat me, slapped me and made me lie in the dirt.

"On the farm it was really hot, but we were not allowed to take water with us. One day, I fainted from being dehydrated. The officer thought I was faking it and beat me even though I was not conscious.

"One of the most traumatising instances that I still remember to this day was when one of our unit-mates tried to hang herself because she could not take it anymore, I think, and I understand why.

"Luckily, another unit-mate noticed that she was acting strange and followed her to the restroom and saved her. Seeing her on the ground almost dead and every one of us crying around her is something that I will never forget.

"This was a normal or typical day in the camp; it was really just slavery. And I think they made sure to let us know that it was slavery. I remember one instance when we were filling the jerry cans and our officer, who was standing about a hundred meters from where we were, had a cup in his hand and it fell. He then called me and ordered me to hand him the cup from the ground. I was baffled but had to do it regardless. Food was very limited, and we had to rely on parents sending us enough food to survive."

Allae lasted an entire year at the SAWA camp during which time she was not allowed to see her parents. She completed her high school education in September 2015.

"After we completed the matriculation exam, we had three more months of military training in the camp before getting the matriculation results," she said.

"A typical day during this time would begin, by us waking up at 4am with a whistle then we'd clean our dorms and restrooms until 5am. Then there would be fall-ins (military drill) and, we then would go running for up to an hour. At 6am we were given ten minutes to eat our breakfast."

After hours of gruelling military training, compulsory exercise, pointless manual labour and political indoctrination sessions, the day ended for Allae and her classmates at around midnight.

"This would be an ideal day, when we were lucky enough to not be punished throughout the day for silly reasons. They would also blow a whistle sometimes suddenly at about 2 am to do more fall-in," she said.

"On weekends we would go to farms owned by the officers. There was more mandatory exercise or cleaning, or we would go to collect wood and stones or do other menial tasks. They would occasionally make us to move an avalanche of stones from one place to another and move it back again to where it originally was.

"There was a time when we were asked to collect chickpea sized sand grains for about three hours nonstop for no reason. We always were asked to do these kinds of strange tasks when we had nothing else to do or were simply taking a rest.

"I was lucky enough to pass my matriculation exam and qualify for tertiary education. So, then we were taken to the Eritrean Institute of Technology. This was a place also run by the military and life there was not much better than at SAWA. We had classes in the morning and in the afternoon, we worked for the military elite, cleaning their quarters and working on farms, doing weeding and other hard work," she said.

Allae said the there was also a lot of harassment by military officers at the college as life became increasingly intolerable.

"We were under the control of the military. Every hour of our lives was controlled. One day in 2016, I couldn't take it anymore and I tried to escape. But I was caught and detained. I was held in a prison cell for two weeks," she said. "In May, after I left detention, the military ordered all of us students back to SAWA for extra military training."

But while waiting to be sent back to the SAWA camp, one night Alla and group of friends managed to escape from the college campus.

"It was 20 kilometres to Asmara, the capital, and we walked all the way through the night. I was determined I was not going to go back to SAWA. I phoned my uncle and he came to meet us and helped us. I hid in my uncle's house for four weeks until he arranged for people smugglers to take us to Sudan."

Allae and her fellow escapees spent an arduous and tense nine hours hidden in the back of a truck to reach a town called Teseny from where they faced a 150km dangerous and difficult trek to safety, through harsh countryside and with constant threat of discovery and arrest.

"To escape, we had to walk at night and hide and sleep during the day to avoid the Eritrean border patrols. We knew that if we were caught, we would go to prison and the soldiers were ordered to shoot-to-kill if people tried to escape after being stopped. We walked for four days and nights and finally managed to get to Kassala in Sudan. From there we were helped by local people who took us to the UNHCR camp at Shagarab. We told our stories to the UN and were given refugee ID. But we couldn't leave the camp and living conditions there were also difficult."

There were instances of Eritrean troops snatching people from the camps and local militia groups had been known to kidnap Eritrean refugees and sell the on to human trafficking gangs.

"It was a scary place and not safe. The idea of going back to Eritrea was frightening so we decided to run away from the camp and go to Sudan's capital Khartoum," she said.

The group was taken to a secret place by the people smugglers where they waited hearts-in-mouths for their families to pay the smugglers by credit transfer before they were released.

"After a few hours of driving, we reached Khartoum and were taken to the house of the people smugglers' boss. My sister Zizi was already in Khartoum and I called her so she could collect me."

Meanwhile, Yara — ten years older than Allae — had made her way to Khartoum earlier but under similarly traumatic and tortuous circumstances.

"I fled Eritrea to avoid having to go into forced military training. I remember two or three weeks into the school year in Year 11, soldiers arrived at our school," Yara said.

"It was 2005 and these soldiers surrounded our school and randomly picked 35 boys and 14 girls from grade 11 to go with them. I was one of them. Everyone freaked out. We weren't due to go to the SAWA camp until the following year and I still don't know why we were picked out."

Over the following weeks Yara and her classmates faced brutal and inhuman conditions.

"I remember they took us to a strange city we hadn't seen before where we stayed for three days. After that they took us to a very bad prison which was an hour and half from the Sudanese borders. They took us to a prison in Keren, we spent three days at the prison with little food and water and with no explanation as to why we were detained or how long we would be detained in the prison. They also refused to let my parents visit me at the prison. We were beaten and abused by the military officers and there was no medical help for when detainees got sick.

"After three days we were transferred to Teseney prison. The prison was basically a camp and we had to work in the bush from early in the morning until night time. The prison cells were basically freight containers. It was very hot, the prison was overcrowded and there was limited food. If you didn't wake up when they knocked, the soldiers would throw water on you, slap you and push you and roll you in the mud and dirt. Sometimes we were beaten with sticks — and we'd have no idea why. We were in a desert area but we were allowed to shower only once a month. Also, there were no proper toilet facilities," she said.

After more than six weeks enduring the terrible conditions, Yara and a few friends decided to take their fate into their own hands.

"I was in a group; myself another girl and three boys. We decided we had no future if stayed. One day, we were being watched by just one guard so we saw out chance and we ran. And we ran and ran and ran and ran. At times we hid behind stones and trees and we walked at night and hid during the day. Each of us had only the clothes we were wearing.

"Our parents didn't know where we were but we made it to a place near Kassala. There we found a local tribe who helped us; they showed us the way to Kassala. When we got there, we thought we were free, we were safe," she said.

During their tumultuous journey some of Yara's group became separated.

"With the help of some local people, I tried to find my classmates. I was with my friend Aster but I still have no idea what happened to the boys we were with," she said.

"Aster knew some people who lived in Kassala but I had no one. She called them and I went with her to stay with her people. From there people smugglers were paid to take us to Khartoum."

After re-establishing contact with her family in Eritrea, Yara faced a new set of dilemmas about her future.

She was able to gain an Eritrean passport through friends in Asmara who bribed government officials. And was supported by an aunt living in Australia who sponsored her to go to university in India in 2006.

"I studied at a junior college in Hyderabad and completed years 11 and 12. I graduated in 2008 and applied to go to university. I graduated in pharmacy in October 2012. Graduating was one of the happiest days of my life," Yara said.

"But after that I couldn't stay in India because my visa had expired. I could not go back to Eritrea because I had fled and would be imprisoned without trial and eventually I would face indefinite national service if I returned," she said.

Yara had no other option but to return to Sudan.

"My siblings supported me to find a house and I found a job in a pharmacy where I worked for two years."

In 2016 Allae arrived in Khartoum after her own epic journey. But despite the joy of being reunited with her sister, Yara's Eritrean passport expired and she was unable to get a new one.

"I ended up with no ID at a time when the Sudanese government was doing a lot of round ups of illegal immigrants," Yara said.

She was forced to quit her job and move to the refugee camp at Shagarab, leaving her sister to stay with friends in the city.

But in 2017 conditions in the camp had deteriorated significantly with food shortages and a lack of hygiene.

"The situation in the camp was difficult. One day I would go hungry and the next day I would eat," Yara said.

"There were also Eritrean military people in the camp posing as refugees so they could snatch people who opposed the government and take them back to Eritrea. I realised I had to find a way out. So, I paid what little cash I had left to people smugglers to take me back to Khartoum. I worked in a pharmacy and at the same time we applied to go to Australia as refugees. At the time, things were getting worse in Khartoum. There were anti-government demonstrations and violence on the street.

"One day my sister went out to get Injera bread and some soldiers started shooting in the street. It was no longer peaceful so, again, we needed to find a better life."

Allae and Yara arrived in Melbourne in July 2019, sponsored by family members already living in Australia, under the Australian government's

Community Support Program (CSP).

Yara had waited five years for resettlement while Allae waited three.

"After years of waiting in limbo in Sudan, we were finally able to come to Australia and start new lives. It was one of the best days of our lives and we are very grateful to be here," Allae said. "But even though I'm now in a safe place, I still have nightmares."

Allae is studying Information Technology at Swinburne University and Yara has been studying Community Pharmacy.

Both have been active in volunteering as they work to establish careers in Australia.

About Eritrea

Eritrea has been a one-party state ever since the liberation forces attained independence 26 years ago.

It has never held a presidential election. All the governors, mayors and other political leaders are members of both the military and the ruling People's Front for Democracy and Justice Party.

The regime relies on force and a large network of informers to report on dissidents. The international NGO Human Rights Watch says Eritreans are subject to arbitrary arrest and harsh treatment in detention.

"Eritrea has had no national elections, no legislature, no independent media and no independent non-governmental organisations since 2001. Religious freedom remains severely curtailed," the group said.

In 1993, after 30 years of violent conflict, Eritrea achieved its independence from neighbouring Ethiopia. Until 1942, Eritrea had been an Italian colony and was run by Britain after the Italian forces were defeated during WWII. In 1952, it was annexed by Ethiopia, officially as part of a UN-sanctioned federation.

Successive Ethiopian governments attempted to suppress independence movements.

A Marxist government was overthrown in 1991. At the time, Isaias Afewerki, the leader of the Eritrean People's Liberation Front (EPLF), was an ally of Meles Zenawi, the leader of the Ethiopian People's Revolutionary Democratic Front, an alliance of rebel movements that were based in various regions and accepted the idea of Eritrean sovereignty.

Eritrea became a sovereign state in 1993. Afewerki became its president, and the EPLF became the People's Front for Democracy and Justice (PFDJ), the nation's only political party.

Meles went on to become Ethiopia's Prime Minister. Afewerki and Meles later fell out, and a brutal war was waged along the border in the late 1990s. Both sides lost thousands of soldiers.

In 1994, the Afewerki government introduced a compulsory "national service". Every year, 10,000 to 25,000 high-school students are recruited, and they undergo military training.

For all school pupils, Year 12 takes place here. The service has no time limit, however, and the women and men drafted do not know for how long they must serve. Some are not set free before their 50th birthday.

Human Rights Watch says that "several thousand people" flee from Eritrea every month to escape the national service.

CHAPTER 8

TRAGEDY, ART AND THE HUMAN CONDITION — A REFUGEE'S PERSPECTIVE

For Bosnian-Australian artist Saidin Salkic surviving the horrors of Srebrenica has fuelled a cathartic and intense passion to create art.

The filmmaker, poet, writer and visual artist says witnessing the worst mass killing in Europe since the end of World War II still lives with him.

"For me Srebrenica is the present. I live with that every day," Saidin said.

He was 12 years old when Bosnian Serb troops overran the United Nations declared "safe area" where he, his mother and sister, and thousands of other Bosnian Muslims had sought refuge in July 1995.

Tens of thousands of Bosnian Muslims had fled the Bosnian Serb army and were being protected by 600 lightly armed Dutch peacekeepers in the enclave in eastern Bosnia.

But on July 6, the Bosnian Serb army advanced. They took some of the Dutch soldiers hostage and demanded that the Bosnian Muslim fighters hand over all of their weapons in return for safety.

The Serbs then took away males aged 12 to 77 for what they said would be interrogation. The first killings began just two days later and, over five days, more than 8,000 Bosnian Muslims were killed.

Also, 23,000 women and children were forcibly deported amid widespread reports of rape and torture.

As his family tried to board a bus to leave the camp near Srebrenica, soldiers ordered Saidin to one side.

"My mother realised I had been taken away and she turned around and she started screaming, pulling me away," Saidin said. "They pulled their guns out. They said 'shut up we are going to kill you'. And then one of them said 'he is too young he can go'."

But Saidin's 33-year-old father was not so lucky. He was captured as he attempted to hike a forest trail to the town of Tuzla.

His execution was recorded on the infamous "Skorpions video" which emerged in 2005 finally confirming the murderous excesses of the Bosnian Serbs.

"On SBS News in 2005, I saw the execution of my father in the video with five other Bosnians," Saidin said. "He was wearing the same blue shirt I saw him wearing last. He was executed last. He was made to pull the bodies of other people who had been executed into the bushes."

The video was instrumental in bringing the leaders of the Serb forces — including Bosnian Serb commander Ratko Mladic, President Radovan Karadzic and the paramilitary leader known as Arkan — to justice.

It became the "smoking gun" — the final, incontrovertible proof of Serbia's part in the Srebrenica massacres — when it was shown at the UN's war crimes tribunal for the former Yugoslavia in The Hague.

The brutal tape shows the execution of six Bosnian Muslim prisoners, four of whom were under 18. The beaten prisoners, hands bound, are shown lying face down in a lorry. A guard kicks one in the head. They are ordered off the truck, told to lie down and, in a later clip, shot in the back while standing.

The first four to die are ordered to walk forward, one by one, and then shot. Then the hands of the last two — one of them Saidin's father — are unbound and they are told to carry the bodies to another spot, where they are also shot.

Saidin is still haunted by those times.

"Everybody I ever played with never came through. Never came back. And these were all just boys — 10, 11, 12, 13-year-olds," he said.

After years in refugee camps the Salkic family settled in Australia in

2001 making Melbourne home.

Now a father himself, Saidin says his 7-year-old daughter Sevdah has brought his family joy. He has been able to find solace in his art while also carving out a career as an extraordinary experimental filmmaker, poet, songwriter and painter.

His work has been exhibited widely, including in Melbourne, Sydney, Adelaide, Brisbane, Sarajevo, Belgrade, Gratz and Cork.

His first film *Karasevdah: Srebrenica Blues* is a meditation on the nature of suffering and the possibility of reconciliation.

The film was launched by Marcia Langton in 2007 and co-produced by Paul Komesaroff and the Global Reconciliation Network.

Another recent work, a 40-minute film entitled *The Arrival of the Phoenix*, was featured at the Adelaide Film Festival and the Wyndham Learning Festival.

Despite the trauma he has witnessed, Saidin says he has fond memories of his childhood.

"I am aware of the discourse of memories everyone reaches into and tries to speak about. I will try and do it my way, as a poet that I am, in the midst of it all. Growing up was full of childhood laughter, winter slides and barefoot summertime runs down the hills of Bosnia. The excited runs down towards the river. There at that mountain stream, hidden among the summertime leaves, I once saw my childhood friend, Dzemo fishing. He never survived the Srebrenica genocide. I still remember seeing him that day. Many years later I made my first film *Srebrenica Blues* and I spoke about the lost boys from my childhood. Based on that film, one of the greatest Indigenous artists of all time Tracey Moffat, sponsored the making of my second film, *Konvent*."

He says his experiences of conflict have meant that he grew up quickly.

"A boy can grow up quickly. I felt I did grow up quickly. Instead of laughter I started hearing the sounds of shells flying through the air, as I was running through those same fields, this time in fear, hoping that we'll get somewhere safe, before the inevitable explosion."

He says the death of his father changed his life forever.

"You can never be comfortable talking about things like that. It completely changed my life. I became the man I am, in a moment of time. My father was one of the most beautiful humans that ever laughed under the clouds, truly. And some of us have more right upon that word "truly" than others. Some of us have fought and suffered for it more than others.

"There is a shrine in Bosnia for my father, where many people gather every year. I have said this in many national and international interviews, for many years I made the art for the glory of my father.

"Then, when my daughter Sevdah was born, I released that I was making it also for her. In the midst of it all, I must have been making it for myself too," he said.

Saidin says his interest in art came slowly but ultimately overwhelmed him.

"The art invaded me gently, but with immense intensity. I became one of the most prolific artists of my generation, with such wide and intense output. I have made ten avant-garde films, some of them have been called masterpieces by different people. I suddenly felt wide awake. It is impossible for me as an artist to practice the sacred medium and not to feel the responsibility of evolving it and making it more relevant than it was, before it became mine."

He says that art has been an anchor in his life providing meaning and solace.

"I have always said: 'family is family and art is friends'. To me, it has proven itself as such. You have used such a specific and beautiful word 'solace'. That is what peace is in a way, it is silence. And I have learned to treasure it profoundly. Art has shown me the way in this, our Australian society."

He says he still maintains emotional connections with his homeland.

"It has always been so important to me that my people know what I am doing, with what passion and with what intensity. This, because of them knowing who I am, from where, what I do, and under what circumstances of history, it has always been important for me that they know I am working hard."

Saidin says he is now focused on making a contribution to art and society in Australia.

"We are here, in this moment of time, in this beautiful land we have the privilege to call our own. I am in a way in the epicentre of it; at the heart of the artistic and with it social and moral evolution forward.

"I am working hard to have the art I make further influence the social streams of our society. We bare the great responsibility to advance our Australian society in every moral specificity that we can.

"I would like all in this society, including the 'immigrants' and those who consider themselves 'Australian' to know that we are all the same, we have the same foundations, rights and with it responsibility.

"All the great historically documented achievements happened after the great migrations. We are that society now. Many things are being achieved. I am a part of it. The culture is something that constantly evolves, changes and grows, and all the migrant communities are an equal part of it.

"I need them to feel proud and equal and with it; responsible to the present and to the future of our great society. With every step we take, we must try to make it more just, more relevant and more beautiful for all of us to enjoy."

CHAPTER 9
BONDED TO THE BUSH

Karen-Burmese refugee Kaw Doh Htoo was forced to flee his home three times. Chased out by the Burmese army who burned down his village, he spent almost a decade in a refugee camp in Thailand.

Now, after rebuilding his life in Australia he has become a leader and inspiration to his community and has opened his own business, while also finding a slice of heaven in rural Victoria.

"I am a Karen from Burma but I had to leave my country because of the civil war there. The Burmese military burned our villages and we had to flee," Kaw Doh said.

"Three times I was forced to leave my home and finally we had to leave the Karen state — the place we call 'Kaw Thoo Lei' — our mother land. We crossed the border into Thailand and we were sent to a refugee camp. I lived in the Nu Po refugee camp in Thailand for nine years. We were given food for our families living in the camp but the Thai authorities would not let us go outside of the camp. So, I could not find any work in Thailand to give my family a better life. Life in the camp was hard. We lived a temporary life there. We did not know what the future would be or whether we would ever be able to go home."

Kaw Doh says he won the lottery of life when he was accepted by Australia for refugee resettlement.

"I was lucky that Australia gives opportunities for refugees from around the world to settle here. And the Karen Organisation sponsored me and my partner to leave the refugee camp and come to Australia," he said.

He has been in Australia for 13 years with his wife Eh Tha Dah Paw and they have four children. When they first arrived in Australia, the family lived at Werribee in Melbourne's west.

"I started learning English with AMES and later I became a community guide with AMES helping other refugees settle," Kaw Doh said. "We helped lots of people in Werribee and Geelong to find houses and jobs and get their children into school. I also was a volunteer with the Karen Organisation in Victoria."

Kaw Doh was part of program to settle Karen-Burmese refugees at Nhill, in western Victoria, which is emerging as a model not only for refugee settlement but also for the revival of struggling rural towns.

About 180 Karen refugees have been settled in Nhill, attracted by jobs being offered by local poultry producer Luv-a-Duck.

Local leaders say the arrival of the Karen has breathed new life into the town, bringing economic benefits and enriching its cultural life.

An economic impact study on the program found the program had added more than $100 million and 150 jobs to the local economy over a decade.

"I decided to move to Nhill with my family because there was an opportunity to find work and buy a home. At first five of our people started working at Luv-a-Duck in 2010. There were lots of challenges but we worked hard and never gave up. Now, there about 180 Karen people in Nhill and we have made it our home."

Over ten years, the Karen have settled well in Nhill, attracted by employment and affordable housing prospects.

"When I first moved to Nhill, ten of us lived together in a house we called 'the big house'. In Nhill, we started to organise a dancing group for Harmony Day and we celebrated Christmas and the Karen New Year. Now, each year we celebrate the Karen New Year and we invite everyone in Nhill. We Karen have a community volunteer group team and we have been working with the Hindmarsh Shire Council and the Learning Centre to host the New Year celebration events. We invite the whole Nhill community to share our New Year celebration with us and we put on a show of our traditional songs and dances. Then we share a Karen meal," he said.

Kaw Doh has also worked to improve the educational and employment opportunities of his people.

"I was thinking about how my people could rebuild their lives and their skills and have better lives and futures in Nhill. So, I went to see Annette Creek at the Learning Centre and we talked about education for adults to improve their skills and knowledge and their communication skills."

The result was the setting up of basic English classes, computer classes and sessions where people from the police, the hospital and other agencies came and talked to the Karen people about life in Australia.

In 2016 Kaw Doh decided open a Karen grocery shop so his people could buy Karen specialty food and the things they need without having to leave Nhill.

"Most of our Karen people are working at Luv-a-Duck and usually they travelled to the city every weekend to buy what they need. It's a long way to go," he said. "I thought it would be good to have a shop here in Nhill so that people do not need to drive so far. One of my friends from Hindmarsh Shire Council helped me apply for an ABN and the other things you need to set up a business. Another friend helped me to understand how to order the products and how to manage in the shop. I buy products from Melbourne but also vegetables from the Nhill community garden. The business started very small but it is growing.

"I would like to thank our Australian government. We are all grateful for everything provided to our Karen refugee migrant families in Nhill and elsewhere. I miss my home. I miss the jungle and rivers. But life is good here. I like living in Nhill and it's a good place for my family," Kaw Doh said.

CHAPTER 10
"MY KIDS NOW HAVE A FUTURE"

Nelson Venturini's journey to Australia began on a day in 2009 when he was kidnapped by a criminal gang in his native Venezuela.

Driving home after work one day, his car was intercepted and blocked by an armed gang who abducted him and threatened to kill him.

The Telecom engineer was forced to hand over his car and empty his bank account before he was released.

"I was in my car on my way home when it happened. There was a gang of gunmen — I don't know who they were," Nelson said.

"They took me away and threatened to kill me unless I gave them all of the money I had. At the time I had been planning to get married so I had saved money to buy furniture and things for the house — but I lost it all. They took all my money and my car but after one night I was released. It was just one night but it marks you for your whole life.

"So, I started to research migrating to different countries but I had to carry on with daily life and in the meantime my wife and I had two kids.

"Then in 2014 there were so many protests with people on the streets. People were complaining about the government but many of them were put in jail. During the protest, I saw how the army were hitting students who had no weapons. They killed some of them for no reason. I worked in a tall office building which had large windows so I could see how the police and army were treating people during the protests… it was very bad.

"I was just thinking about my kids and that was when I really decided I had to leave. The protests made me move even faster to migrate. I thought about what would happen to my kids if they grew up in that environment.

"There is a very difficult situation in my country. It so dangerous, so many people die every day and politically it has been very unstable."

Nelson said he remembered a time in Venezuela when the nation was safe and prosperous.

"As a child I remember we left our house unlocked and we played in the street with our neighbours. My father went to work and my mum stayed home with the kids. We had everything we needed. People in Venezuela would travel overseas maybe once a year and it was a good period of my life. But Venezuela went from being one of the best countries in Latin America in which to live to one of the worst. But we didn't realise the situation was changing so fast."

Venezuela has more recently been mired in corruption, military dictatorships and violent crime; and, since the 1980s, economic decline.

The most recent round of instability began in 1998 when Hugo Chavez was elected president amid disenchantment with established parties. He launched the "Bolivarian Revolution" that brought in a new constitution, socialist and populist economic and social policies funded by high oil prices, and increasingly vocal anti-US foreign policy.

In 2013, the inflation rate reached more than 50 per cent a year and the National Assembly gave President Maduro — who succeeded Chavez — emergency powers for a year prompting protests by opposition supporters.

Crime in Venezuela is endemic, with violent crimes such as murder and kidnapping often increasing annually.

A UN report attributed crime to the poor political and economic environment in the country, which has the second highest murder rate in the world.

Crime increased rapidly during the presidency of Chavez due to the institutional instability of his government. By the time Chávez died in 2013, Venezuela was ranked the most insecure nation in the world by Gallup.

Crime has also continued to increase under President Maduro, who continued Chávez's policies that had already disrupted Venezuela's socioeconomic status.

In 2015, crime, which was often the topic Venezuelans worried about the most according to polls, was the second largest concern behind only food shortages.

The majority of all crime in Venezuela remains unpunished according to Venezuela's Prosecutor General's Office, with 98 per cent of crimes in Venezuela not resulting in prosecution.

According to the UN, more than 5.5 million Venezuelans have left the country since the start of the country's crisis and more than 2.5 face food insecurity.

Nelson said he had no choice but to leave his homeland.

"I had a good position in a big company in Venezuela but the safety and future of my kids was more important and led to me to decide to leave. Chavez created this experiment where he incited the poor to fight the rich and it created divided society. His policies destroyed the economy. We had inflation and a breakdown of productivity.

"I researched many countries and found that Australia would be a good place to migrate to and Melbourne was a good place to come to in Australia. I had to work hard to get my visa. There were requirements around qualifications, experience and language. I could satisfy the qualifications and experience requirements but I had to work hard in my English language skills so I studied English for more than a year to prepare for the IELTS exam," he said.

Nelson completed a Skilled Professional Migrant Program course with settlement agency AMES Australia and after nine months of searching for a job is now working in Melbourne as a telecommunications engineer with a major international company.

"It's a junior position but it's a professional job and I hope to build my career here," he said.

Nelson says he is enjoying life in Australia but is worried about his mother and sister still in Venezuela.

"They are just surviving and I worry about their safety. But now I have a job I can send them some money to buy medicine and food."

As for his immediate family, life is good, Nelson says.

"I enjoy watching my kids in the playgrounds outdoors. In Venezuela that would not be possible. Here they have a future and they have a lot of opportunities and they can decide what they want to do in life. I am very happy and grateful to the Australian Government for giving migrants the opportunity to have a good life here. In Venezuela, you spend a lot of time thinking about how to survive, how to get food and medicine and how to stay safe. Here, I can improve myself, do better at my job and contribute something back to society."

CHAPTER 11

"THE GAME OF THEIR LIVES" — HOW THE AFGHAN WOMEN'S SOCCER TEAM LIVED TO PLAY AGAIN

In September 2021, the Afghan women's soccer team should have been competing in Asian Cup qualifiers taking on other national teams from Central Asia and the Middle East.

Instead, they were fleeing their country and seeking safety across world as part of the coalition nations' evacuation of vulnerable people out of Kabul as militant Taliban fighters took control of the city.

The sportswomen feared for their lives and their futures under the Taliban which has re-imposed harsh restrictions on women, including a strict ban on participation in sport.

One group of about a dozen players has washed up in Melbourne and are seeking to rebuild their lives and sports careers in Australia.

They are among more than 200 sportswomen — mostly footballers, cricketers and martial arts players — who fled Afghanistan in fear of retribution at the hands of the Taliban.

One player Zahra (not her real name) spoke about the trauma of having to flee her homeland; and of her fears for the women of Afghanistan and her own family members.

Zahra, who is not being identified because of safety concerns for her family, has played for youth and senior national football teams for several years.

She says the team's dramatic exit from Kabul amid bombings, gunfire and human stampedes; and also of the heartbreak of leaving family members and teammates behind to face an uncertain future was the worst week of their young lives.

"The week the Taliban took over in Afghanistan we were very worried. We were scared the Taliban would target us because we were women athletes," Zahra said.

"We heard news they were taking away women athletes, arresting some players and that some other players had been kidnapped or killed in remote provinces."

Zahra said she and her teammates were supported through their ordeal by Khalida Popal, a former Afghan women's team captain and founder of the Denmark-based women's rights NGO "Girl Power".

"Khalida sent us a message to get together a backpack with our basic necessities and a mobile phone and power bank. She told us not to take any documents which the Taliban could use to identify us. We spent that night the Taliban came into Kabul awake, talking and watching the bad news unfold on social media. All night we were hoping someone would come and help us. When we decided we had to try to get the airport, our families were supportive. They were happy for us to go telling us that we were in danger. But we were all worried, in turn, about our families. There were still documents that could identify us and put in danger our families who would be left behind in Afghanistan."

She said that the team had become well known in Afghanistan through social media and media publicity around the matches they had played in five major tournaments staged since 2019 — the last being against Tajikistan at the CAFA Tournament in June.

Zahra said that finally, they got a message from Khalida to take their backpacks and go to the airport. Khalida had organised visas for the group with coalition nations.

"We set off for the airport, most of us with family members who we were hoping would be able to come with us. It was very scary, there were guns firing in the air and lots of people outside the airport," she said.

"We went to different gates and we had to go through Taliban checkpoints. It was really dangerous."

Zahra and teammates were separated in the crowd as they tried desperately to get into Kabul's international airport — at the time, the last bastion of coalition forces in Afghanistan.

"It was very difficult for us. We went to each gate to try to get in but at each gate none of the soldiers knew who we were. We had been outside the airport for 24 hours and no one had come to help us. We started to lose hope."

Finally after 48 hours of looking for a way in the team got a crucial and ultimately life-saving message from Khalida to "go to the south gate".

"I volunteered to go first and find a way in and I promised I would get everyone else in. Khalida had said that 'the Australian military will help you' but just as I approached the gate my phone was almost dead and I could not tell everyone else on our WhatsApp group what was happening," she said.

Just then the suicide bombs went off creating more confusion for the women.

"I got through the gate after three hours and three attempts but just as I did, my phone died so I had no contact outside. Luckily some of our girls also got through and I was able to use their phones tom contact everyone else and guide them to the gate."

But many of the women had to leave behind family members who were not allowed through Taliban checkpoints.

"Luckily our girls were able to go the right way to the gate but it was very difficult and they were lucky to get in. The Taliban were beating people. And the Taliban would not let through people without visas so many of our family members had to stay behind. Our families put us first, they said 'you go now, we'll follow you later'. We were all separated from family members at the checkpoints and most of us didn't get to say goodbye with all the chaos. It was heartbreaking for us," Zahra said.

At the last checkpoint she was kicked and punched by Taliban fighter demanding to know who she was.

"He was shouting at me in Pashtu but I only speak Dari so he got more annoyed. I don't know how, but I made it through to the airport gate."

She said three siblings had managed to get out with her but her parents and other relatives remain in Afghanistan.

Zahra said that once inside the airport perimeter, she helped Australian soldiers identify teammates still outside and help them get across ditches and razor wire to safety.

They spent three nights in a makeshift camp inside the airport in freezing conditions before eventually being flown out to Dubai on a military aircraft.

After nine days at the Australian military's Camp Arcadia in Dubai the team was flown to Australia and into hotel quarantine.

Most have chosen to stay together and settle in Melbourne. They are looking forward to their futures in a new country but still harbouring fears for family and fellow sportswomen still in Afghanistan.

In a recent sinister statement the Taliban said it was "not necessary" for women to be involved in sport and that "Islam and the Islamic Emirate (Afghanistan) do not allow women to play… the kind of sports where they get exposed".

In response, Khalida Popel hailed the evacuation of sportswomen from Afghanistan as "an important victory".

"The last few days have been extremely stressful but today we have achieved an important victory," she said. "The women footballers have been brave and strong in a moment of crisis and we hope they will have a better life outside Afghanistan. We are relieved that this group of footballers and athletes have been able to leave Afghanistan today. Our hearts go out to all the others who remain stranded in the country against their will."

Zahra said that she was heartbroken that women's sport in her homeland would now come to an end.

"We should be playing Asian Cup qualifiers right now but instead all we have worked for and hoped and dreamed about has been swept away. Most of us were studying at university at home but now women in Afghanistan will not be able to do that. The Taliban said they would respect women. But there is no respect for women, they have been removed from cabinet and Afghanistan is going backwards into the past. It's shameful."

Football remains a symbol of hope for the future for the women and most are playing in a team representing Melbourne City Football Club in a local Melbourne league.

"Some of our girls have been traumatised. They have seen so many bad things. But I think football will help us get over these bad times," she said.

"I certainly want to play again to build my future and make connections. We are not going to dwell on the past. We are going to do our best to be role models and to be strong for ourselves and for women still in Afghanistan.

"We heard that there's a professional women's football league in Australia. That is really exciting."

CHAPTER 12
REFUGEE'S JOURNEY FROM MAELSTROM TO MEDICINE

Batool Albatat fled the first Gulf War and Saddam Hussein's brutal regime with her family as an 11-year-old girl.

Put by people smugglers aboard a leaky boat piloted by a 14-year-old boy, the family and their fellow travellers became lost in the Indian Ocean and expected to die.

Rescued from their floundering craft, the Albatats were eventually accepted by Australia as refugees.

Now, Dr Albatat, 31, is saving lives herself as a surgical resident at Melbourne's Northern Hospital. But twenty years ago this summer she was stranded in the middle of the Indian Ocean with 130 other desperate asylum seekers drifting aimlessly. Water and food had run out and the teenagers driving the leaky fishing boat had no idea what they were doing even before the engine broke down. They were only saved when an Australian Coast Guard vessel chanced upon them and prevented them from disappearing into the vast expanse of the Indian Ocean.

When Dr Albatat's family fled Iraq in 1991 and crossed into Iran they had with them little more than the clothes on their backs.

"My parents just had to pack up and go, they just wanted to save their lives and their kids," she said.

Her father was an engineer in the southern oil city of Basra and the family enjoyed an affluent lifestyle.

"We grew up wealthy, so it was a shock running away, leaving everything we had behind and being suddenly poor, crammed into a tiny house with my cousins, uncles, and grandparents."

A few of their extended family made it to Australia as refugees and Dr Albatat's father decided to follow them to give his family a chance at survival. However, people smugglers demanded thousands of dollars for each family member and they could only afford to take the two youngest boys. At the last minute, Dr Albatat's grandfather decided she was too young to stay behind and scraped together the cash to fund her trip.

"That decision changed my life dramatically,' said Dr Albatat, the fifth of seven siblings. "Saying goodbye was heartbreaking as we didn't know if we would ever see them again. We heard that so many people died trying to get to Australia, but it was our only chance."

The family's escape from Iraq was shrouded in secrecy.

"Getting out of Iraq was dangerous. If my parents had been caught, they would have been killed," Dr Albatat said.

"My parents travelled separately to Iran. My Dad had stayed behind longer to gather some belongings and when we reached Iran, he wasn't there. We didn't see him for a few months. We didn't know anyone in Iran and we didn't know how to speak the language. My mother had no nappies for the babies and no milk but the Iranian people helped with the basics and food."

Life in Iran was difficult for the family with no official status the children were not allowed to attend school and work for Dr Alabatat's father was difficult to come by.

"But the Iraqi people built an Arabic school for the Iraqi children. So, I did grades one to four at the school and I learned Persian on the street," she said.

Eventually, the family was able to pay people smugglers to get some of the family out of Iran.

"Myself, my two younger brothers and Mum and Dad left Iran, but my older brother and two older sisters stayed behind."

The family flew to Malaysia on forged passports and then to Indonesia where they were moved around by smugglers every day to avoid the police.

"Every day for three months we were told we would get on the boat tomorrow, only to be told we couldn't. We ran out of money and for weeks lived on only rice. Sometimes we added sugar to make it easier to eat. Then for the last few days we had nothing to eat. There were many other Iraqi people who had been waiting longer, or they paid the smugglers all their money who then took it and ran off."

Eventually they were taken to a beach under the cover of darkness and hid huddled in silence for hours until the boat arrived.

The tiny fishing boat was crammed with 60 asylum seekers and looked like it would be lucky to make it off the beach.

"The boat shouldn't even have been at sea, it was old and falling apart," Dr Albatat said. "As soon as the engine started people started vomiting from the fumes and clouds of smoke the old engine was belching out along with the rocking from the sea."

Dr Albatat woke after a few hours' sleep in the middle of a storm only to be told they were heading back to shore.

"It was a tiny ship in a big storm, there was big waves and rain, we didn't know where we were going, and the boat was sinking," she said.

For two weeks the refugees were marooned on a tiny forested island off the coast of Indonesia living with the local inhabitants.

"Everyone lived in tree houses because it was too dangerous on the ground where there were crocodiles and snakes. The local people took turns guarding everyone else through the night so the animals didn't kill them. My mother was crying the whole time about leaving my brother and sisters behind and Dad felt like he'd brought his family out there to die but he had no choice as we couldn't go back and he'd already given the smugglers all his money," she said.

Another boat that left Indonesia about the same time sank and many asylum seekers drowned, with word soon reaching refugees still on shore.

"After we left Indonesia, none of our family knew if we were dead or alive and when they heard a boat sank they started organising funerals for us," Dr Albatat said.

Finally the smugglers arrived with a bigger boat but crammed more than 130 people on to it so it was just as crowded as before.

Soon after leaving Indonesia, the captain left the boat, leaving it to be piloted by two teenage boys aged 14 who, as minors, would not face jail sentences in Australia.

"Our lives depended on two boys who barely knew what they were doing. We had no idea where we were or if we were going the right way — all we could see was water around us," Dr Albatat said.

"By the second day the boys were lost and we were almost out of water, we shared out what water was left and we tried to make it last. We could only drink a cap-full every few hours.

"Everyone felt like they were going to die and were preparing for the end. Some people got desperate and lit fires on the boat at night hoping someone would see them.

"A storm was coming and the boat was leaking. On the third day a plane flew over but it didn't see us. Everyone lost hope and was crying and praying because we were sure we were going to die."

On the fourth day the engine broke down and the rickety boat was left drifting far out sea at the mercy of the wind and waves.

Finally the Australian coast guard arrived and it transpired the boys steering the ship were headed for the middle of the Indian Ocean where everyone would surely have died.

The boat was towed to shore and everyone on board was sent to the Christmas Island detention centre.

Dr Albatat remembers the camp as harrowing, "like a prison", surrounded by hopeless asylum seekers, including children, waiting to learn their fate.

"Many people we met on Christmas Island were there for years and had no idea when they would be allowed to leave," she said.

But the Albatat family's claims for refugee status were accepted in just three months and they were sent to Melbourne where her cousins lived.

Not knowing a word of English, Dr Albatat at first struggled to fit in at school in suburban Australia.

"I only had my cousin to talk to. But when I learned enough English I was able to make friends and sit with everyone else," she said.

Soon after, they got Australian citizenship and were able to bring her brother and sisters to Melbourne and reunite the family in 2008.

"It was an amazing relief to see them safe in Australia after seven years. My mother struggle for so long and she was overjoyed to have the family together again," she said.

Dr Albatat says that initially school in Australia was difficult.

"But I studied hard because I didn't want to let down my family. They had gone through amazing hardship so that we could have futures — so there was not time to waste."

By the time Dr Albatat finished school, her English was good enough to pursue higher education. She earned a biomedical science degree from La Trobe University before studying a Doctor of Medicine at the University of Melbourne, graduating in 2017.

She completed an internship at The Northern Hospital and has just started her third year as a surgical resident.

"I love working here, everyone has been very supportive and kind to me," she said. "The staff is very multicultural, from all over the world and I get along well with everyone. I've never had any problems being a Muslim."

Dr Albatat said she feels a debt of gratitude to Australia and its people who welcomed her with open arms

"I'm so grateful to have been welcomed into Australia. I wouldn't be where I am today without the opportunities it gave me. I feel a sense of privilege to be here and have this opportunity that so many people, including my parents and my other siblings that we left behind, haven't had. Therefore I feel an obligation to do well. Because of what I have been through, because of what my parents have been though, I have this strong sense of obligation."

Dr Albatat said she also felt great gratitude to her parents for providing her with a future.

"There were so many scarifies to get us to where I could achieve my dreams. I couldn't waste that opportunity; there was no time to waste or room to mess around, no room to have fun, no room to have a party," she said.

"There was expectation that so much had been put in and invested in me; that we the younger generation are the hope of the older generation. They didn't speak English, so we are their voice. They couldn't use their degrees so we became their degrees. They could not achieve the success they wanted here, so we are that success for them in so many, many ways. And even thou there were many restriction along the way, they always find alternatives."

But she said her success is bittersweet.

"My siblings who stayed behind in Iran for those first years missed out on the opportunities I've had to get a good education. The journey has been tough, but I feel privileged to be a doctor now, and to be able to help people at the most vulnerable time of their life."

She says her experiences as a refugee have made her stronger and a better doctor.

"The trauma and the experiences I've been through have taught me a lot and made me more resilient. My experiences help me in my work; help me to be more compassionate and do as much as I can for people from non-English speaking backgrounds and people, who have suffered trauma in their lives. Everyone has a different story and you never know what people have been through."

CHAPTER 13
HOSPITALS AND HAND GRENADES: A REFUGEE DOCTOR'S JOURNEY FROM HELL

Afghan trauma surgeon Abdullatif Stanikzai's life changed forever the day three wounded Taliban fighters were brought into his Kabul hospital.

The men had been shot and captured in a gun battle with police who demanded they be kept alive so they could be interrogated.

Despite the best efforts of Dr Stanikzai and his team, the men could not be saved. And just days later came a chilling message from the dead men's comrades: "you killed our people, we are coming for you".

From this point Dr Stanikzai was catapulted into a cascading series of violent terror attacks. He was shot three times; members of his family were murdered and he was finally forced to flee for his life.

But ironically, it was after he had been resettled in Australia as a refugee that he came closest to losing his life when a botched skin graft operation left him in hospital with septic shock and septicaemia.

Now, slowly recovering from his ordeals, he is desperate to get his remaining family members to Australia and out of harm's way; and he hopes to resume his medical career. But the COVID-19 pandemic, his own health issues and bureaucratic inertia are proving to be frustrations.

"I had a good life in Afghanistan despite the security situation. I had a good job that I loved, helping ordinary people. And I was engaged to be married. But this is my life, this is what I have been given," said a phlegmatic Dr Stanikzai.

He had worked for about five years as a trauma surgeon at the Civilian War Victims Kabul Emergency Hospital, a facility funded by the European Union. He also worked as a volunteer medico with the Red Cross.

"We had a contract with the government to treat anyone who was injured; local civilians even some of the terrorists like the Taliban. At times we treated US and British civilians who had been injured in some of the attacks in Kabul. As a doctor I would give my number to some of the people we treated so that I could follow up with advice about their recovery. Many of these people lived far away from the hospital and it was difficult for them to travel. I didn't know it at the time but my number was being shared and one day I got a call from a group of insurgents who were fighting against the Afghan government."

The group was the Haqqani Network, a guerrilla group formed during the Soviet-Afghan war which later became affiliated with the Taliban and Al-Qaeda. The group is believed responsible for several terror attacks on western embassies, kidnappings and for a truck bomb explosion in Kabul in 2017 which killed more than 150 people.

"They asked me to come and work with them to treat some of their fighters who had been wounded. I told them I could not do that because I worked for ordinary people not terrorist groups," Dr Stanikzai said.

"They said 'we'll kill you and attack your family if you don't work with us'. I contacted the intelligence police who told me to tell them if I was approached again."

Shortly after this incident in 2012 Afghan police brought three terrorist fighters who had been wounded in a gun battle into the hospital where Dr Stanikzai was on duty.

"The police said they were senior members of the terrorist group and they wanted they kept alive so they could be interrogated. The three were very badly injured and had little hope but we did our best to save them. Unfortunately they died."

Shortly after Dr Stanikzai received a chilling message from the group's base in Pakistan saying "you killed our people".

"It was a clear threat that they would targets us — all of our eight-person trauma team at the hospital was at risk. It was frightening but also insulting because as doctors we would never deliberately harm a patient. We had done our best to save them but all three had very severe wounds."

Dr Stanikzai talked to his superiors about the threats and the team was given security protection and a driver.

Sometime later, the doctor and some of his team were preparing to go home after a long day in the operating theatre. As they left the hospital they walked into a hail of bullets.

"I was hit in the leg, the chest and the abdomen and the force of the bullets threw me backwards and I cracked my head on the wall behind me," Dr Stanikzai said. "Somehow I survived but a colleague, who was another doctor, and the driver were killed. I was unconscious for a long time and when I woke up I didn't understand what had happened because I had suffered had trauma."

Dr Stanikzai said the attack made him realise how vulnerable he was.

"When I was recovering I was thinking that as a doctor this kind of violence was the opposite of what my life was about. I found it hard to understand how we, who were dedicated to saving lives, could be targeted by these people in such a way."

After a period in hospital Dr Stanikzai was discharged and returned to his work performing surgery on civilian victims of Afghanistan's intractable conflict.

One day he was preparing to go home to the village where his family lived to celebrate a festival but was held up because of a string of emergency surgeries and didn't make the festival.

That night the terrorist group attacked his house in the village, killing his father, his uncle and younger brother.

"They were looking for me and asked where I was. They threatened to kill everyone if I wasn't handed over. My uncle, who was a policeman, although not armed at the time, fought with them and was killed. Then they shot my father and my brother in front of my family," he said.

"They said 'where is the doctor? Show us your son or we'll kill everyone'.

"Just then the police arrived and the terrorists escaped — but not in time to save my father and uncle and my brother."

After the attack in the village, Dr Stanikzai's remaining family — his mother, two sisters and four brothers — moved to the relatively safer environs of the capital Kabul.

"For a while we were secure but then one day when I was walking in the city, I was shot in the chest with a silenced gun. I never saw the gunman and I never heard the shot," he said.

When, in 2014, Dr Stanikzai once again recovered from the latest gunshot wound, his superiors advised him to leave the country.

"I was given a passport and documents and I went to Dubai and then to Indonesia. The Afghan Government supported me to live in Indonesia. I could pay rent and I even managed to get some work as a doctor with the Red Cross helping other refugees," he said.

After five years In Indonesia, where he was linked to IOM and then UNHCR, Dr Stanikzai was given status as a refugee.

Given the choice of going to the US, Canada or Australia, he chose Australia.

"I had a friend living in the US, in Texas, and he said 'don't come here, it's just like Afghanistan, there are guns and bandits everywhere'," Dr Stanikzai said.

Before leaving for Australia, Dr Stanikzai had a motorcycle accident and suffered a small injury to his leg. On arrival in Adelaide in April 2019, he was referred to a plastic surgeon for skin graft surgery on the injury. Ironically, this was a procedure Dr Stanikzai had himself performed successfully dozens of times.

The surgery led to an infection and Dr Stanikzai ended up unconscious in hospital with septic shock and septicaemia. He endured 13 further operations to try to repair the damage.

Eventually his case workers at refugee settlement agency AMES Australia transferred him to Melbourne in April 2020 where more sophisticated treatment was available.

After spending a month in the Royal Melbourne Hospital, Dr Stanikzai partially recovered. He still is only able to walk with crutches and has suffered mental health issues because of his ordeal. He has been linked to the National Disability Insurance Scheme (NDIS) and is receiving support.

"I am doing physio and rehabilitation and I'm working on my mental health," he said.

Now, Dr Stanikzai's priorities are to bring his family and fiancée to safety and to find a pathway to be able to resume his medical career. His worries about his family have heightened since the Taliban took control of Afghanistan in August 2021. Several member of his family have since disappeared and his family had reported people being killed all over the city in apparent revenge killings by the Taliban. Also, there were reports of women and young girls being taken by Taliban members.

"The Taliban came to my family's home and broke in. They used some kinds of explosive to break the door down. They smashed the house up, breaking everything and beating my family members. They blindfolded and tied up my elder brother and his two sons — they are 18 and 16 years old. My brother had been in hiding since the Taliban resurgence and had only just come back to our family home. But the Taliban took them, put them in the toolbox of the truck and took them away. We are very worried."

He said the incident sent one of his two-year-old nephews into a fatal fit.

"My family said the boy started crying and that he died later. I asked what he died from, but they could not tell me. They could not bury him, they had to leave his body in the house."

He said the remaining dozen or so member of his family, including some children, then went to Kabul's international airport to try to leave the country.

"My family went to the airport but they could not get in. It was being guarded by American soldiers who would not let anyone it. My family said they had problems with the Taliban but no one would listen. They spent two days at the airport and they had no food or water. They said an American soldier gave them some water and told them to go home."

Dr Stanikzai said the Taliban had not observed their promise to eschew revenge attacks and respect the rights of women and minorities.

"My family said the Taliban had been attacking many houses and there are bodies all over the city. They also said that women and young girls were being taken. The Taliban said they would forgive people but they lied. They are attacking houses and they are killing people."

Many Afghan community leaders in Australia have spoken of their fears for the future of the nation and for lives of people who may suffer acts of revenge by the new Taliban regime.

Thousands of Afghans across Australia hold grave fears for their family in Afghanistan after the events of the last few days.

The Taliban has seized control of most of the country in a lightning campaign that took most observers by surprise.

The Australian government closed its embassy in Kabul in late May 2021, and the last Australian troops left the country in June after almost 20 years of military intervention alongside the United States.

CHAPTER 14

SAVING ABSAAR — HOW AUSTRALIA'S REFUGEE SYSTEM SAVED A BOY'S LIFE AND RESCUED HIS FAMILY

Minutes after touching down at Melbourne's Tullamarine Airport in November 2019, four-year-old Absaar Ahmad was carefully transferred to a waiting ambulance and rushed to the city's Royal Children's Hospital.

The boy was suffering from holes and blocked arteries in his heart, a condition that had gradually worsened over the five years he and his family spent as refugees in Malaysia.

On arrival, Absaar was in a critical condition, malnourished, weak and turning blue. His parents Anwaar and Asifa feared the worst.

Absaar underwent emergency open heart surgery. His doctors said they were able to save him only because he was brought to the hospital in time.

The now seven-year-old has recovered and is attending school; and his family are well settled in Melbourne's northern suburbs.

"It was a frightening time for my family. My son was very sick. He was blue and not moving," Dad Anwaar said. "But thanks to the Royal Children's Hospital he is much better."

Absaar's life was effectively saved by Australia's sophisticated refugee settlement system and the hard-working and dedicated staff who run it. The Ahmad family were due to be settled in Adelaide in November last year but timely detective work by case workers, armed with details of Absaar's condition, unearthed the fact that there were not adequate medical facilities in South Australia to treat him. Thanks to this timely intervention, the family's arrival point in Australia was switched to Victoria, a move that effectively saved the boy's life. Key to this outcome was the involvement of medical specialists and hospitals and the arrangement of emergency transport from Melbourne airport.

The family's first days in Australia were challenging and overwhelming because of Absaar's condition and his recovery from serious and complicated surgery.

Absaar's case manager William Paul said the family had limited language ability and no social connections on arrival.

"The family was significantly socially isolated and were experiencing culture shock. But we were able help the family to overcome these barriers and get back to normality by providing them with a comprehensive intervention," William said.

Absaar is now doing well. He is healthy and attending kinder; and the family has settled well in the Broadmeadows area, in Melbourne's north.

"My son is very well now. He has come back to normal and is attending kinder," Anwaar said.

Anwaar and Asifa are grateful to the doctors at the Royal Children's Hospital and to the Australian government and people.

"We now have a safe life in Australia and we have a healthy son. We are very thankful to the doctors and everyone who helped us at the Royal Children's Hospital. And we are grateful to the Australian government for giving us a new home," they said.

Before arriving in Australia, the Anwaar family had spent five difficult years as displaced persons in Malaysia, where they had fled to from their home in Pakistan because of the persecution they suffered as members of the minority Ahmadiyya Muslim sect.

The Ahmadiyya sect of Islam has been subject to various forms of religious persecution and discrimination since the movement's inception in 1889.

Ahmadis are considered non-Muslims and heretics by many mainstream Muslims; and they are routinely subjected to persecution and systematic, sometimes state-sanctioned, oppression.

Pakistan's constitution also deems Ahmadis to be non-Muslims and deprives them of religious rights. About 2.5 million Ahmadis live in Pakistan, the largest population in the world.

Hundreds of Ahmadis were killed in the 1953 Lahore riots and the 1974 Anti-Ahmadiyya riots. The May 2010 attacks on Ahmadi mosques, infamously known as the "Lahore Massacre", resulted in the murder of 84 Ahmadis in suicide attacks.

Once Absaar had stabilised post-surgery, Anwar and Asifa were determined to find employment as soon as possible.

Anwaar was provided with employment related orientation and training through Australia's refugee settlement program and he secured a job at a chocolate factory within few months of arrival.

Even though he was retrenched due to COVID-19 restrictions, Anwaar was re-engaged by the same employer and recently was promoted to an even better role which he hopes will become a permanent position soon.

The family feels they have fulfilled their aim of living together as a family and being financially independent with their employment and education outcomes.

While Anwaar is in full-time employment, Asifa is learning English and establishing social connections with other mothers from her community.

In Pakistan, Asifa was a leading women's cricketer who played at the national level. She is hoping to join a women's cricket club in Melbourne as well as to gain employment once she has improved her English.

Absaar's story shows the value of well-resourced settlement programs. Australia has a very generous and sophisticated refugee settlement program that is among the highest per-capita intakes of any permanent settlement country in the world. The program provides support for refugees to integrate and become economically independent and socially connected, and is a reason Australia enjoys high levels of social cohesion. Many refugees who have found their way to Australia have suffered torture or trauma, some have lost everything they owned or held dear and others have lost family members.

Australia was one of the earliest signatories to the 1951 United Nations Convention on Refugees. The convention stemmed from WWII and the Holocaust and it was designed so that we would never again see people at risk of death or persecution turned away by countries where they sought sanctuary. The convention lays out and bind signatory countries to the legal notion of non-refoulement — which means that a nation cannot forcibly return someone to a country where they may be subjected to persecution.

CHAPTER 15

OF COWS, WOMEN AND WAR — THE JOURNEY OF A REFUGEE SONGSTRESS

Multi-talented South Sudanese singer Ajak Kwai came to Australia as a refugee fleeing the brutal and interminable civil war in her homeland.

Having re-established her life here, Ajak is sharing through her music her own story and the rich culture of her people. She presents a weekly show on PBS radio and has been touring widely across Australia.

As a Dinka woman, Ajak has used singing and storytelling to help maintain her connection to her people and their cultural traditions as well as assuaging the trials and trauma of being a refugee forced to flee everything she held dear.

Ajak says that as a child she had a speech impediment and avoided talking. But her memory and natural musical talent made her the songwoman of her village and a custodian of her people's stories.

When war broke out, her fiancé was forced to join the military. He was killed. Subsequently, she lost her father, two brothers, two nieces and several cousins and her village was attacked and razed by rival militia.

"The militia came to my hometown and killed everyone," she said. "Some people died of hunger because they looted the town, people were hiding in the bush, and they had no food."

Luckily for Ajak, she had already fled to the city with her uncle.

"My village has gone. There is nothing there to go back to," Ajak said.

Despite the devastation, Dinka culture remains a central pillar of Ajak's life.

"I come from the Sudan. My culture as a Dinka person is very unique. We are nomads, very strong-minded people and sometimes people don't like us," she said. "In Sudan, we did pay a very huge price because of the war which was absolutely devastating. My country South Sudan was absolutely devastated by the war. Many people were killed or forced to flee their homes. So the pride, it dies. People become miserable, people have lost their homes, they've lost their animals."

But Ajak has found solace in music at the most difficult times in her life.

"Music helped me a lot in my life. My mum died when I was quite young. My father had another wife, so I did not really live with my father for a long time. I was withdrawn and I did not talk very much. When I became a refugee music helped a lot because I would write a lot of poems and sing. Singing and music gave me hope and an outlet for my feelings. We were refugees in Cairo for a long time, for eight years. It's a long time to be staying, doing nothing. We could not find work and our future was uncertain. The music, the singing, the writing it really helped me in my journey from the Sudan to here."

Ajak was almost lost to Australia as many of her fellow South Sudanese refugees were drawn to attempt to get to the US.

At first she was suspicious of Australia's colonial past, but she says she has felt welcome here since arriving in 2001.

"The group of people I was with wanted to go to America and I was going to go with them. And at the time we heard that Australia had killed its black people a long time ago and that they don't like black people at all.

"I went to the Australian embassy in Cairo and we met young Australian people at the embassy and they were very good looking young people but me and my cousin — we joked 'Oh my god, they so look ugly because they are so mean'," she laughs.

Ajak says she sees similarities between African and Australian indigenous cultures and is moved by the plight of some aboriginal communities.

"I travelled around Australia in 2011 playing at festivals and I heard a lot of indigenous musicians and met the people in communities," she said.

"Actually the Indigenous cultures here are very similar to our African culture. The stories are similar you know. I saw people sitting under the trees and that made me think about home. And that's how I came to write my stories because I could see the pain in the eyes of these people. They were sitting there. There are no jobs and they are struggling. But these are beautiful welcoming people. So to be able to see them like that it remind me of the sadness I felt at home during the war. To see some of the problems Aboriginal people have is so sad because there is no war here. It's good to know where people come from. It's good to know about what it's like for other people in their lives. I'm very proud of my people because I think they are very good people and the novelty of the Dina people, I love that. And everyone in South Sudan, I feel for them."

Ajak was originally settled in Tasmania but moved to Melbourne in 2007 drawn by the city's vibrant music scene.

She has performed constantly since them and has been a regular at the WOMADelaide festivals in recent years.

Her *Of Cows, Women and War* theatre show was released as an album in February 2016, establishing her reputation as a soulful songstress.

It's a rich mixture of African-soul melodies and tells of her extraordinary journey from being exiled from her home, to gospel singing in Cairo and starting afresh in Melbourne.

Recently she released her fifth studio album *Let me Grow My Wings*, fixing her place firmly in the Australian music landscape.

She has been touring Victoria and engaged with some of Victoria's best producers and musicians to bring life to an eclectic collection of twelve self-written songs which reflect her observations, influences and connections since arriving in Australia.

CHAPTER 16
REFUGEE SETTLEMENT AT NHILL — TEN YEARS OF SUCCESS

It's close to sundown and the birdsong reaches an end-of-day crescendo as a small group of people carrying hoes and rakes drift among the garden beds pushing and prodding as they tend the crops.

The tranquillity is palpable as the gardeners expertly pull out uninvited weeds — and harvest plump tomatoes and fiery chillies along with strange looking greens and gourd-like vegetables.

This is the community garden at Nhill, in western Victoria, where at the end of every day a group of Karen-Burmese refugees come to tend the plots where they grow traditional foodstuffs that cannot be had in the local IGA supermarket.

The quiet, lush garden on the edge of town is a long way from the teeming refugee camps of the Thai-Burma border where most of the Karen were born or spent decades of their lives.

The garden is part of an extraordinary initiative which has seen the Karen refugees resettle at Nhill, in Victoria's Wimmera District.

The settlement program, which has just reached a ten-year milestone, was effectively begun by John Millington, OAM, who in 2009 was General Manager of local poultry processer Luv-a-Duck.

With a lack of local labour to facilitate the company's expansion, Mr Millington turned to settlement agency AMES Australia to see whether there were any refugees willing to relocate to Nhill.

After arranging for a group of Karen to visit the Luv-a-Duck plant and Nhill, four workers were hired.

Nhill has since become a centre of resettlement for Karen people, who now make up about 10 per cent of the population, or around 240 people in all. Most began their Australian lives in the Melbourne suburb of Werribee, before settling in the town from 2009. Now there are more than 160 Karen working at the plant, on local farms and in local businesses.

"We learnt very quickly that it was important that the partners and kids of the workers were involved. We knew that they had to be looked after, engaged and connected to the community or the whole thing would fall over," Mr Millington said. "It was also important that the local established community was on board, so we made sure they understood what was happening."

Now, ten years on, the settlement of the Karen is bedded down and they are part of the fabric of Nhill's community.

CEO of the Nhill Learning Centre Annette Creek, who also has been instrumental in supporting the settlement of the Karen, says it's "not a big deal anymore".

"We've got to the point where the Karen are part of our community and our town and it's not a point of discussion," she said. "And that's exactly what you want. It's a really good symbol of how well the integration here has happened."

Over the ten years, a generation of Karen children have grown up in the town. Apart from the way they look, they are indistinguishable from Australia-born kids in town. Ms Creek says they are represented among the town's netball teams and other sports groups.

"At the school presentation night recently, there was an equal split among the award winners between Karen kids and local kids. Ten years ago in Nhill, the Karen community stood out — now we're a true multicultural town."

Although the effort to settle and integrate the Karen at Nhill has had its challenges, Ms Creek says it has been "absolutely worth it".

She says the Karen are now significant contributors to the local community although the process to reach sustainable settlement was much harder than she imagined at the start.

"Really the success of this was built on the good will of people. At first a smallish group put their hands up to support the Karen but the wider community has also been prepared to embrace the newcomers."

Ms Creek says the whole experience has been personally rewarding.

"Every day, as I meet and connect with the Karen community, I'm always touched by their resilience and their ability to make a go of things here. If we can give them the opportunity to make new, fulfilling and sustainable live for themselves, why wouldn't we? I love seeing them succeed and thrive. I enjoy seeing them achieve milestones like buying a house or getting a job they didn't think they could do. It's incredibly rewarding to know that you are making a difference in people's lives."

The settlement of the Karen has spawned some other interesting projects.

One of them is "Paw Po", which means "little flower" in Karen, a social enterprise that makes colourful and artistic products that combine contemporary design and creativity with traditional, loom-woven fabrics. The business, which has a shop on Nhill's main street, provides the opportunity for Karen and other women to develop and share skills, prepare for employment and connect with each other and the community at large. It grew out of job ready classes at the learning centre being attended by Karen refugee women.

Ms Creek said Paw Po was part of the Learning Centre's strategy to build skills in the area and especially empower women which won Diversity Innovation Award in the 2017 Victorian Learn Local Awards.

"It's been great for the ladies and also good for the town. We really just followed the ladies' lead as they wanted to do something with their own fabrics and we understood their desire to work with their fabrics," she said.

One of Paw Po's mainstays is Karen woman Asoe, a qualified seamstress who has started a clothing alteration business out of the shop.

Asoe came to Nhill two years ago from Bangkok and helps the other women make a range of dresses, bags, kids' clothes, scarves and other fabric goods.

"I like it here. It's quieter than Bangkok and there are opportunities here that Karen people in the camps cannot take," she said.

An economic impact study carried out by Deloitte Access Economics in 2015 found the resettlement program at Nhill had resulted in positive outcomes for the refugee families and added almost 100 jobs and more than $40 million to the local economy.

Over five years, 70.5 full time jobs were created, representing a three per cent increase in total employment across the district, and $41.5 million was added to the Gross Regional Product.

In the months following the completion of the report, another 27 jobs were created in and around Nhill.

The study, titled 'Small Towns Big Returns – Economic and social impact of the Karen resettlement in Nhill', found that like many other regional towns, Nhill faced a declining working-age population, the resultant loss of services and amenities had flow-on implications for the economic and social prosperity of the town.

It found that a declining population in the town and a very low unemployment rate were key factors in the resettlement.

"In particular there was a need for labour to support expansion of Luv-a-Duck, the largest local business, and driven by a combination of economic and humanitarian motivations, Luv-a-Duck management identified the Karen as potential employees," the report said.

"Through a staged recruitment and resettlement process, the Karen community now comprises approximately 10 per cent of the Nhill population, including significant numbers of working age adults and families with young children. Furthermore, labour force participation linked to this population increase is high."

The study also identified significant social outcomes stemming from the resettlement program, including: the arrest of population decline; revitalised local services and increased government funding, and an increase in social capital across both communities.

A second study marking ten years of the settlement program at Nhill found that the total economic impact from the regional resettlement of the Karen population on the economy of Nhill and its surrounds is estimated to have been $105.5 million, with an associated impact on employment of an extra 156 jobs and 230 people added to the population.

It also found that because of the youthful demographic profile of the Karen population, the Karen labour force will continue to grow over time, adding to the productive capacity of the region in years to come.

The report found the resettlement of the Karen at Nhill has been sustained over a decade because of the region's attractiveness as a settlement location for this community.

It identified key factors in this success, which include: a welcoming host community; sustainable employment, appropriate housing and employment and educational opportunities for families.

The Karen at Nhill have experienced improved standards of living, including home ownership, and greater opportunities and career pathways for young people, and the settlement has seen Nhill enriched culturally by the presence of the Karen.

John Millington says the positive economic and social outcomes have moved beyond the Deloitte report.

"What has happened here in Nhill with the arrival of the Karen has gone to another level and everyone is benefitting," he said. "There are new families arriving from the camps on the Thai-Burma border and we now have about 27 Karen home owners in town. Four Karen nurses are employed at the hospital and we have Karen employed in local businesses and farms. But just as importantly, the presence of the Karen has enriched the rest of us."

The positive social impact of the Karen being here continues to be extraordinary.

"We are a small rural community that has embraced and opened its hearts and minds to the Karen," Mr Millington said. "This has enriched the community through exposure to another culture. It has made Nhill a better and more interesting place to live and it's made us all better people. It never started out as a grand plan. It was just something that happened. It's really grown into something very special and Marg (John's wife) and I are really humbled by the success it has had. This was not just our doing. It was picked up by the whole community and everyone has benefitted.

"The Karen have found peace and happiness and a place to call home — and they've got safety and security almost for the first time in their lives. The community has benefitted in that the Karen's presence has helped our community stay strong and build on the things that went before like sports and service clubs. And obviously businesses and the local economy has benefitted," he said.

Marg Millington says she is proud to have been part of the program.

"We're proud to be part of a humanitarian mission that has had astounding outcomes in helping so many people and that belongs to our small township," she said.

With regional settlement of migrants and refugees high on the federal government's agenda and with many regional communities actively seeking to attract more migrants, there are important lessons that can be learned from the experience at Nhill.

Annette Creek says that early investment in settlement and integration could pay dividends in the long term.

"The big issue for us in the beginning was the lack of services, or funding for services. We relied heavily on volunteers and community support and that made it hard," she said. "There is so much grass roots work to be done in preparing for a migrant community to settle in a small town and I would advise communities to put their hands up early and say 'we need help here'. It can be done but you do need to put your heart and soul into it. You need to think outside the square and be resourceful and look for ways to make things work. Every town is unique with a unique set of circumstances but you will always need the good will of the community to make things work. If communities — and even the nation as a whole — puts resources in and invests early, we can achieve sustainable success that can have a lasting impact into the future."

One of the beneficiaries of the investment made at Nhill is Po Tha. Po moved from Toowoomba to take up a job at Luv a Duck. He said it was the sense of community and the welcome that attracted him.

"In Toowoomba there were not many Karen, there was no feeling of community for me. I heard about Nhill and the Karen community here. So I came with my family. In just a week, we have made friends. My kids have made friends and I am volunteering to help in the garden.

"We feel at home here. We feel at peace. The people here -— all of the people not just the Karen — are friendly and welcoming. I think my family will have a good life here," Po said.

CHAPTER 17
REFUGEE'S LONG JOURNEY TO SAFETY

When Celian Kidega fled South Sudan at just 17, he was setting off with his classmates on a long and hazardous journey on foot through jungle, war zones and across national borders.

It was the start of an even longer journey that has seen him find a new home in Australia, raise a family and work to help others displaced by conflict and persecution.

Celian is the co-founder and Director of Magwi Development Agency Australia — a foundation working on issues of education and female empowerment in South Sudan and Uganda.

The foundation, which was created in 2018, has founded a school in Sudan that now employs 16 teachers full-time, has 550 students and has graduated three groups of students with Year-12 equivalent certifications.

It also sponsors 25 women in Ugandan refugee camps, where it campaigns against forced marriage and assists women with the costs associated with breaking such arrangements.

Back in his homeland, it was Celian who began his journey of displacement under the care of a woman.

"The rebels attacked and took the villages first, making things very insecure, so that is why people such as me were displaced to the city where the government could provide some safety," Celian said. "From the village to Juba, my sister went with us and took her younger brothers and looked after us."

Like many others, the family were caught up in the early stages of one of the longest and bloodiest of Africa's many post-independence conflicts.

Over its twenty-two-year duration, the Second South-Sudanese Civil War claimed the lives of more than two million people, and displaced more than four million at least once, and sometimes repeatedly.

"The first war was from 1955–1972, the second war was from 1986–2005, between the government and the rebel Sudan People's Liberation Army (SPLA)," Celian said.

"The main cause of the war was that the South Sudanese people felt very marginalised by the mostly Islamic government in Khartoum, who took away South Sudanese autonomy. So, many people joined the rebels leading to a high-intensity war and the displacement of many people.

"These issues have their roots in the negotiations for independence (from joint British/Egyptian rule), which led to the marginalisation of the south with poor systems of health and education," he said.

While the rural areas' isolation made them a first easy target for the SPLA, the group's ambitions and brutality were always destined for the cities too.

"The rebels started attacking Juba, bombarding the town almost every day, and the government had changed the policy so that everybody had to learn in Arabic, making it very difficult for those who hadn't learnt it. Sharia law was also being implemented, and there was the policy of forceful military training after completion of high school. I participated in organising a group of my schoolmates to leave. It was organised by a group of students. It was an organic movement among the people. I was a part of that group, and this put me in a lot of danger, and as a part of that my father was arrested after I left. But we got out of Juba successfully."

Starting in Juba, South Sudan, Celian's journey by foot took him through more than 500 kilometres of jungle and rebel-held territory to Uganda. Most of the group never reached their destination.

"From Juba we cut through the bush into the villages, making our way towards the border. At first, the main threat was from the government because it didn't like people defecting to rebel territory. We were very fortunate in our group — there were people who tried to follow us only an hour later, many were arrested and we don't know what happened to them.

"There was a lot of hardship walking, with the lack of food and water, just walking through the bush and drinking any kind of water we could get on the roadside. As we walked, we saw that all the animals had left the jungle because of the fighting."

Despite keeping to the villages, the group was unable to avoid detection.

As the death toll for both sides steadily climbed, the SPLA began to utilise all possible sources for potential soldiers, including children. When the student-group's journey was waylaid by the rebel group they were at first met with kindness in the form of food and water. Yet the rebels' true intention for the boys was forced conscription, to put guns in their hands and psychologically mould them from students into killers.

"The whole group was conscripted by the rebels, but I escaped," Celian said. "I was successful in escaping because my elder brother was in the rebel forces, so he was responsible that we got in the truck to the training camp. It was not a good place to be, people were being asked to kill and they were being put in danger.

"The night when the leader came to take people in the truck, those people snuck me out of the camp with them and three friends of mine. They brought some military raincoats and put us in them, then had us walk with another soldier carrying a gun and we passed through the gate and out. We walked out like we were going for a smoke, but it was a sneak-out," he said.

Celian managed to slip through the cracks, and instead of beginning his training with the rest of the group, he was back in the jungle, focused once more upon the safety of Uganda.

This time, he and his friends were successful, and were taken from the border area to the UN refugee camp in Adjumani.

Here, he recounts, the conditions were comfortable, and he was able to feel safe again with a small house on a block of land where he could grow his own vegetables and mingle peacefully with the local people while receiving support from the UN.

But it was not a home, just another temporary encampment liable to the volatile political shifts of the region at the time, and thus Celian was once again forced to flee the activities of an armed militia.

"The political situation was very unstable. It's not a new thing, most of this area of this Africa has spent a lot of time in war — since the '60s there has always been war in one of those countries, and it flip-flops. One will always be in chaos. There is always war in one of those areas, because of people in power trying to gain influence for the resources, supporting rebels instead of marketing for peace or another approach."

He said the Lord's Resistance Army, a heterodox Christian militia group, would attack people along the road between Kampala and Adjumani.

"Because of that it reduced the movement and communication and it caused starvation, because the UN vehicles could no longer come with the food. We lost our support and life became quite difficult in the camp," Celian said.

He then journeyed to Kenya, to his next place of stable residence the infamous Kakuma refugee camp, which at the time housed refugees from seven different armed conflicts in the region.

Today, it is the world's biggest refugee camp, with more than 185,000 residents. Compared to the lush jungle of Uganda, however, the arid and harsh climate of the region gives the refugees there little means of supporting themselves.

"Kakuma is a desert, so you rely purely on the UN to distribute what you need," Celian said. "In Uganda it is a jungle, so it was very easy to grow food yourself to supplement what was provided, but in Kakuma if no food was distributed you did not eat, and water was itself a constant issue."

With the malnutrition and ethnic violence that too often characterises Kakuma, it is common for people to spend years there, stagnant as they await the peace they need to return home.

Celian did not become of one these people. While the rebels had intended to make him a soldier, he remained a student. To rebuild his life, he turned once more to education.

Through the Dominican Order of Friars, Celian begun training in religious and philosophical studies at the Consular Institute of Philosophy in Nairobi.

Here he learnt English and became a missionary, skills which would directly inform his eventual success in trans-national activism as well as migrant community engagement here in Australia.

Like most refugees at the time, the invite to come to Australia came from a cousin, who agreed to sponsor Celian's migration to join him in Perth in 2002.

At the time, Australia's migrant services were just a fraction of the network available now, and the onus was instead upon the migrant's sponsor to integrate the individual.

"The sponsor had more responsibility for 202 visas then, my cousin took me to Centrelink for registration and everything," Celian said. "The only thing available from settlement providers were beds and everything, which I didn't need. When I came down here, I enjoyed the support of a catholic group called a group of brothers. Through the Church, they gave me a job counting all the money on a Monday to be taken to the bank just because I was a member, four weeks after arrived, and helping out with the church."

He then moved again to study social sciences at the University of Tasmania, majoring in Public Policy and Human Resource Management.

It was here that he was first engaged in community work. The University of Tasmania utilised Celian's lived experience towards remedying a specific issue they were facing — keeping young migrants engaged in their studies as they struggled with issues of integration.

Celian presented to them as an equal, with shared experience. Here he found a passion for community engagement.

"I would go house to house interviewing people about their settlement experience," he said. "I enjoyed this work. When I finished in 2006, I wanted a job anywhere within three months. I did not mind where, but this was my mission, to be employed quickly and begin to work. I achieved this with the Australian Refugee Association in South Australia. I worked there for eight years in several roles. When I started in 2006 it was as a case worker, then a training officer, then as an elite training officer in cross-cultural communication, competency, profiling and public speaking."

With time and opportunity, Celian has continued to steadily develop his capacity, working across various organisations as he looked to contribute.

"Eventually, I became involved with AMES Australia in 2017," he said.

He now works as Case Manager with the migrant and refugee settlement agency in South Australia.

"I was also very involved with the Rotary Club. I was the president there until a year ago, as a business director for all community interactions and local projects, contacting team leaders and directing them in their activities."

For his contribution to the Rotary Foundation of Australia, Celian has been awarded the Paul Harris fellowship — just recognition for a man who has directed his own hardship not into anger but to alleviating the hardships of others.

Amid all his achievements, however, he is most proud of the Magwi Development Agency Australia, which he founded in 2008 to help his countrymen and women back home, while also connecting his current work to his own struggles and his identity as a South Sudanese refugee.

"Our focus is on 18 and under, but there are instances where we work with young women as well on the aspect of education. We work with women who are facing violence, and we campaign to end forceful marriage. There have been instances where there is an individual who has been forced into marriage, and we pay the compensation to the family to bring her back to school," Celian said. "There must be payments made to free her from this situation, and here we find the opportunity to help her."

For Celian, his mission through Magwi will always be in tribute to the care he received from his sister, and the knowledge of what she would miss out on because of her gender.

"My sister stayed in Juba until the war ended and has now returned to the village. Her name is Luci Anyiri. During all this time of struggle and running, my mum has passed away and Luci looked after us. She never got a chance to go to school, so in 2004 when peace was coming to South Sudan, I thought I should contribute something to appreciate and recognise her, and also acknowledge that our culture still doesn't give opportunity to girls."

For Celian himself, today he conducts his philanthropy from his home in Adelaide, where he lives with his wife Naa Koshie, as well as his 15-year-old daughter Esther and 11-year-old son Jeremiah.

After flee king his homeland to find safety, Celian says Adelaide is the first place he has allowed himself to become comfortable since leaving his village as a child.

"I call this place home, we are settled," he says. "We are happy."

CHAPTER 18
REFUGEE POET'S WORK LIVES ON

Maryam Daryos' poems are a poignant rendering of the profound and contradictory senses of loss and hope that are at the heart of the refugee experience.

Her work is even more heart-wrenching in that it was published as the prize-winning entry of an international poetry competition after her death — which came shortly after she gave birth to her first child.

Maryam's poems live on as a legacy for her family and also as a reminder of the growing refugee and human displacement crisis across the globe; and they present an intensely human and microcosmic representation of war, displacement and physical and emotional trauma.

Her book *Souls Covered With Ash* contains 22 poems that viscerally describe the experience of seeing one's family, friends and homeland ripped apart by conflict. But the poems also convey hope and a sense of resilience that transcends the dire news reports and statistics that have characterised the recent wars in Iraq and other parts of the globe.

Maryam's husband Waad Japrita and son Toma arrived in Australia in January 2020. The family fled their home in Mosul in 2016 when ISIS invaded the area in northern Iraq.

As Christians they faced being targeted not just by ISIS but also by newly emboldened Islamic militant groups.

As ISIS swept through northern Iraq, they killed or kidnapped Christians, forcing them to convert to Islam. Villages and churches were burned down. In the face of this, the family fled to Jordan and applied to come to Australia as refugees.

Life became more difficult and untenable in Jordan as they were unable to work and had little support so, reluctantly, they returned to Iraq in 2018.

Maryam became pregnant with Toma. The pregnancy and birth put pressure on her already weak heart, which had a hole in it.

After the birth Maryam suffered heart failure, she went into surgery but died 12 hours later. Waad was devastated but had to carry on for the sake of his new-born son.

He was finally granted a visa to come to Australia in 2020 and was settled in WA, coming to Melbourne three months ago to be with his mother, who had arrived in Australia earlier.

Waad said that his wife worked as an English teacher in Iraq.

"She studied a Diploma of Education in English and did other English courses because of her passion for the language and poetry," he said. "She took part in many competitions and she won first prize in a competition run by a Swedish aid organisation with her book. Part of the prize was to have her book published but sadly, it was not published until after she passed away. My wife's dream was to leave behind the problems in Iraq and come to an English-speaking country like Australia to continue with her passion for English and poetry and to give her son a better life. I am trying to live her dream for her and to give Toma a better life just like she dreamed. She would want me to carry on and give Toma all the opportunities that Australia offers and I plan to do that. I hope that Toma can one day get a sense of who his mother was through her poetry and understand what a wonderful person she was."

Waad also has an artistic background. He completed a Diploma in Art in 2009 and worked as an actor, performer and photographer in Iraq.

He is now studying English and caring for Toma while living with his mother in Melbourne's north.

"I hope to be able to resume my artistic life here in Australia and work in the arts," he said. "But life is good here for us. We are grateful to

Australia. We are safe and Toma has a bright future ahead of him. He can do anything he wants. That would not be possible in Iraq."

But Waad said that one day he hoped to take Toma back to Iraq so he could see his mother's last resting place.

"When it is safe, I will take Toma back to his mother," he said.

In the preface of Maryam's book, she wrote:

> *Thank you for picking up this book. Let me just start with a fair warning: reading it may cause you some discomfort.*
>
> *Life is not always easy for a Christian in Iraq. For me poetry is a way to let these sorrows escape my heart. Writing helps me to sort things out, to prevent anxiety and stress from taking the upper hand. Formulating my troubled feelings gives me hope.*
>
> *My name is Maryam Daryos. I teach English and Art and picked up writing poems in 2009 when I studied to be a teacher in Mosul, the city I grew up in. I used to have my own room for writing. I'd light candles to create the perfect creative atmosphere.*
>
> *In 2014, IS came, and like all Christians, we had to run for our lives. We lost a lot, but I kept writing. My poems have become more sombre since then. I try to remain hopeful, but hopelessness is always just around the corner.*
>
> *However, when I look up to the sky I always know there is hope because then I think about Jesus, who has been there for me and has given me His grace all the way.*
>
> *As I'm writing this, I'm pregnant. My husband and I are expecting our firstborn child. Where will this child grow up?*
>
> *Will there be a future for us in Iraq? New hope is growing within me and at the same time new uncertainty is added to our lives. That's how life is when living in Iraq.*
>
> *My wish is that these poems will give you an insight into the suffering of Iraqi Christians. I hope they will help make the world*

aware of those who have no voice. And that, by sharing my sorrows and hope, I can be an example for the hopeless — don't give up, keep loving, and when in doubt, look up to the sky!

I would like to thank God for enabling me to serve Him with my pen, my wonderful husband for believing in me and giving me the strength to carry on, and my family and friends for their love and support.

Among Maryam's poems are:

Lost hope…

No place for me I see
No home to be
Lost every heart beat inside
Even my fake smile has died
Trying to cry
Finding a reason to know why
Oh misery won't you leave me
No hope before my eyes I see
Running around the road of life
To gain some time to stay alive
Wishing a thing from all your heart
Keeps your dreams from being apart.

Sadness no more…

In this life
People laugh & cry
They never stop asking why
Wishing always to die
Looking for love

Looking for hope
In a world filled with misery
Tears oh tears
How can I fight you
Happiness tell me where are you
I don't want to cry anymore
I just want to find a shore
Sadness no more, sadness no more.

CHAPTER 19
NEIGHBOURS STEP UP TO SUPPORT AFGHAN EVACUEE FAMILY

When Afghan evacuee Abdul (not his real name to protect the safety of relatives still living under the brutal Taliban regime) and his family moved into his first Australian home in a quiet street in Glenroy in Melbourne's north, he was not expecting the welcome he received.

The residents of the street — themselves mostly migrants, or the children of migrants, from across the globe — held a meeting to work out how they could help. Then they set to work.

"On the Friday afternoon we moved into the house, we realised the electricity had not been turned on. My neighbour, who had come over to welcome us, said 'don't worry' and he ran a heavy-duty electrical cable over from his property so we would have power," Abdul said.

"I couldn't believe it. Other neighbours brought candles and food for us. The next morning my neighbour made a phone call and after 30 minutes, the electricity was connected — and this was our first day.

"Our neighbours donated furniture. Even though we had been supplied with furniture through the refugee support program, they brought more.

"One neighbour said 'you don't have a microwave, here's a microwave'. Another neighbour has a daughter who is doctor and she offered medical help if we needed it.

"The neighbours have been wonderful. We never expected it. They have done everything for us. They even brought us lunch boxes and school bags for the kids.

"This is what we are seeing in Australia. We never expected it. I'm thinking that our neighbours are very good, caring people. I'm very grateful and we are happy to be in Australia."

Abdul and his family were forced to flee their home and leave everything behind when the brutal fundamentalist Taliban regime took control of Afghanistan last August. As a UN employee who worked with foreign governments, Abdul became a target of Taliban militia.

The family are among hundreds of thousands of Afghans who have fled their homeland since the Taliban seized control on August 15, 2021 amid dramatic scenes.

"I had a great life in Afghan for 20 years in the Karzai era. But unfortunately that has changed with the recent situation and the return of the Taliban," Abdul said.

Abdul worked in operations with the UN office in Kabul.

"I worked with people from Australia, Europe and the US. That is why I was in danger after the Taliban returned. Everyone knew I was working with foreigners," he said.

Abdul said his priority was is his children whom he wants to have opportunities no longer available in Afghanistan.

"I gave all my life for my kids. My priority was to work hard for my kids so they could have a better future. I have three daughters and they were all studying. That stopped when the Taliban came back," he said.

In August last year as the Taliban were retaking Kabul, Abdul received a message from the Australian embassy that he should go to the airport.

He and 16 of his immediate family members immediately headed there. Abdul stood for 11 hours in filthy water in a sewage drain just outside the airport perimeter desperately trying to contact Australian troops so they could get inside.

After finally making contact with an Australian soldier, Abdul was told the email he had received from the embassy was a fake.

"It was crazy and confused. People with legal documents were left behind and other people with no documents at all were able to get out," he said.

The family retreated home and 24 hours later a massive blast just outside the airport perimeter killed 250 people.

With air evacuation over, Abdul moved his family to a provincial part of Afghanistan and he effectively went into hiding.

"For two and a half months I was travelling with some colleagues, staying away from my family," he said. "Then, finally I got a chance to go to Pakistan. And after the Australian High Commission in Pakistan issued us with documents and we were able to get visas to go to Pakistan. But my eldest daughter was stopped at the border because the border officials said there as something wrong with her visa. She had to go back to Afghanistan and she is living with relatives."

The family was able to cross the border into Pakistan and reach Islamabad. The Australian High Commission organised accommodation and flights to Australia. The family arrived in Australia on November 26.

Abdul says he wants to bring his eldest daughter to Australia and is looking forward to improving his English and finding a job.

"I am a worker and as soon as I can I will get a job and support my family. My children will continue their education and my wife wants to get a job because she has never had a chance to work — it is difficult for women to work in Afghanistan. She has a diploma and a bachelor of business administration and she would like to get a job," Abdul said.

Neighbour Hamida Uzel coordinated the efforts to help Abdul and his family in her home just down the street.

"I met Abdul for the first time when he was going shopping with his trolley. He said hello to me and introduced himself as my new neighbour," Hamida said.

"A few days later I was gardening in my front yard and Abdul's kids were playing. They asked if I wanted some help and they helped me plant from succulents around my letterbox. I invited them over for hot chocolate and it was then that I found that they were a refugee family. I asked if they needed anything. They didn't answer but looked at each other — that answered the question for me."

It was then that the neighbours swung into action providing an extra TV for the kids and a dining suite to seat eight — for the family of seven.

"Other neighbours dropped off things at my house and we got everything Abdul and his family needed. I felt like I had to help them. I saw the kids and my heart said that I had to do something. We all need a place to call home," said Hamida, who came to Australia as young child from Turkey in 1970.

Italian born neighbour Nona Rosa has been giving Abdul's children ice creams and other treats.

"They are lovely people. We are lucky to have them living amongst us," she said.

CHAPTER 20
REFUGEE REALISING HIS ENTREPRENEURIAL DREAM

The Baghdad Supermarket in Melbourne's Craigieburn offers ten varieties of coffee as well as a cornucopia of mostly Middle Eastern and Mediterranean foods and produce.

Owner Bashar Audish will blend any of the ten varieties to customers' tastes and he usually throws in a free tub of pickles or spices for regulars.

The store, in a brand-new commercial development among a burgeoning new housing sub-division in Melbourne's north, speaks to the innate hospitality of the Middle-East and also to the optimism and entrepreneurialism of people who have come to Australia from that often strife-torn part of the world.

"I opened the store four months ago in April. The first few weeks were tough because it was a brand-new shop and because of COVID interruptions, but now we are attracting customers and things are improving," Bashar said.

The store now caters to people looking for Middle-Eastern, Italian, Indian and Turkish specialties and Bashar is able to talk to his customers in four languages: English, Arabic, Assyrian and Chaldean.

He arrived in Australia with his parents and sister in February 2014 after fleeing rising violence and insecurity in their homeland.

"We left Iraq because of the conflict and war in Iraq. The security situation in Baghdad became very bad," Bashar said.

"Before 2003, when the US invaded, there was no problem, life was good in Iraq. We had security and the rule of law for everyone. We lived peacefully and no one asked about your religion. But after 2003, people started being labelled as Sunni, Shia or Christian and communities started to splinter into sectarianism. For us as a family, we didn't leave straight away. We waited seven years always saying maybe next year will be better — but it never was."

And as Iraq descended further into chaos, as Chaldean Christians, Bashar and his family became more and more vulnerable to increasingly emboldened militant Islamic groups.

A suicide attack on an Assyrian church in Baghdad in 2010 finally forced their hand.

On October 31, six members of a group called Islamic State of Iraq attacked a church during Sunday evening mass. When the terrorists began killing worshippers, Iraqi commandos stormed the building prompting the militants to detonate their suicide vests. Fifty-eight worshippers, priests, policemen, and bystanders were killed and seventy-eight were injured.

"After that, we realised we had to leave Iraq," Bashar said.

He and his parents and sister sought refuge in neighbouring Jordan but life there was far from easy.

"It was very difficult in Jordan, we could not work and we had no legal standing for three years. But in 2014 we were able fortunately to come to Australia. I am lucky to be here with all of my family. We know of families who fled Iraq who were split up with a brother going to the US and a mother and father going to Europe. We are lucky, we have everyone here in the same city," he said.

After settling in Melbourne, Bashar applied to have his fiancée Zina join him in Australia. They are now married and have two children: Adam, 4, and Lilly, 18 months.

Bashar and his family became clients of migrant and refugee settlement agency AMES Australia but before long he became and volunteer and staff member.

"I had reasonable good English so I decided I wanted to support other refugees who came after me. I have always thought it was good idea to support vulnerable people so I started volunteering to help people from refugee and asylum seeker communities.

"I would take clients to their medical appointments and wherever they needed to go and I was presenting orientation courses for people in their homes and in classrooms showing them how to navigate life in Australia. Then I started working casually as a community guide and as an orientation presenter."

Bashar moved through the organisation working with the accommodation team — finding housing for refugees — and as a client support worker, case manager and finally as a work broker, supporting migrants and refugee to find their first jobs in Australia.

"As a former client and community guide, I knew what was needed to help people on their settlement journeys and I enjoyed the work very much."

But after five months in a new role as a work broker, the opportunity came along to realise his dream of opening a business

"I had a supermarket back in Iraq and also shop that did computer maintenance, printing and design work I've always had it in the back of my mind to open a business here in Australia. But when I first arrived it seemed too difficult and I wasn't aware of all of the rules and what you need to do to open a business. I know my way around in Australia now, I have citizenship and I've got to know more people and contacts. I want to improve and grow the business."

Bashar is speaking from behind his shop counter, his workplace between 8am and 9pm each day.

Above him are a series of pendant lamp shades he designed himself using traditional Iraqi images and motifs. They are bright, colourful and display various Iraqi crafts, music and cuisine — a visual procession of the good things in life.

At least, that's how Bashar sees it.

"Life is good and we are grateful to be here in Australia. I have my shop, my family is safe and doing well and the future is exciting," he says.

CHAPTER 21
UKRAINIAN DIASPORA STEPS UP TO SUPPORT VICTIMS OF THE RUSSIAN INVASION

A large box of 'varenyky' dumplings arrive at an apartment block on the outskirts of Melbourne's city centre. They are being delivered by Darya, a middle-aged blonde woman with an infectious smile.

Darya has baked the sweetmeats as a welcome gesture to a group of Ukrainian refugees who have arrived on flights from Europe overnight and are being hosted in accommodation most recently used to house refugees from Afghanistan.

"It is a small thing, but I felt I had to do something," she says.

The dumplings are emblematic of an outpouring of support from Ukrainian diaspora communities since the Russians invaded their homeland in February 2022.

Ukrainian communities across Australia and the world are rallying to support the people of their homeland as Russia ramps up a brutal military invasion of the beleaguered nation.

Fund raising events are being held across the country to raise money for a humanitarian support effort. And messages of moral support are flowing.

President of the Victorian Ukrainian Association Slawko Kohut said that what was happening in Ukraine was "horrifying".

"We are all worried sick about what's happening in Ukraine. We all have friends and family there. It's very tough," Mr Kohut said. "It is heart wrenching to see what is happening. All that has been achieved over eight years of democracy is in danger of being swept away. We have launched a humanitarian aid effort and we are collecting money to send to Ukraine to support people."

In Melbourne, there have been rallies, vigils and concerts in support of Ukraine held by Ukrainian-Australians across the country. There have also been protests outside the Russian embassy in Canberra.

"We are gathering in what is effectively a group hug. We all have different issues and we will share them," Mr Kohut said.

There are 45,000 members of the Ukrainian community in Australia, 11,000 of them in Victoria.

Mr Kohut has called on all Australians to show solidarity with Ukraine.

"It's important we all do what we can to support the people of Ukraine whether that be with humanitarian support or activism," he said. "In Ukraine today many people are preparing to defend their homeland. We in Australia must be ready to stand in their corner, to support them as we have been doing since 2015."

Mr Kohut said the Ukrainian community was calling on Russia to end the war.

"Putin should stop the war get out of Ukraine. He should also stop telling lies and untruths. He has misrepresented Ukrainian history to support his own unbelievable ridiculous statements. But he's been very clever in how he's planned the war. The world has sat by and watched as things have transpired. Like Hitler he has pretended to negotiate but ultimately had no intention of talking. He put up demands he knew would be rejected and all the while, he was planning to attack."

Nations around the globe, and particularly in Europe, have opened the arms and borders to accept Ukrainians fleeing the Russian invasion.

The UN's refugee agency UNHCR says it expects more than eight million people to flee Ukraine by the end of 2022, more than double the agency's earlier estimate as the conflict drives Europe's worst refugee crisis since WWII.

More than 14 million people have fled their homes in the first four months of the war, including eight million people displaced internally and more than six million who have fled the country, the UNHCR said.

UNHCR had previously been planning to support around four million refugees in the immediate aftermath of Russia's invasion of Ukraine on February 24, 2022, but this was exceeded in March.

"The scale of the crisis, definitely the rapidity of people fleeing, we have not seen in recent times," UNHCR said at the time.

The figures mean that more than 10 per cent of Ukraine's pre-war population of 44 million people fled the country and around 20 per cent were displaced within Ukraine in the two months since Russia invaded.

Women and children make up the vast majority of those fleeing the country, UNHCR said.

Most went to Poland (2.9 million), according to UN data, though many also fled to other nearby countries including Romania (780,000), Hungary (500,000), Moldova (440,000) and Slovakia (360,000).

Another 14 million people were estimated to be stranded in affected areas inside Ukraine or unable to leave.

"The human impact and the suffering already caused by this war are staggering," a UNHCR statement said at the time.

"Families have been torn apart, houses and infrastructure have been destroyed and millions will feel the lasting impact and trauma of war," it said.

Russian forces were accused of targeting civilians and committing war crimes during the invasion, striking cities, evacuation routes, medical facilities and schools.

Areas around Kyiv that have been retaken by Ukrainian troops, including Bucha and Irpin, yielded evidence of executed, raped and tortured civilians, sparking global outrage.

The Australian Ukrainian community traces its antecedents to the arrival of post-World War II refugees from war torn Europe.

Many of these were "displaced persons" and began arriving in 1948. Prior to 1948 only a small number had landed in Australia.

One of the first Ukrainian to arrive was Nicolai Miklouho-Maclay, an ethnographer and naturalist who visited Australia in 1878, and was responsible for the building of Australia's first biological field station at Watson's Bay in NSW.

Today, there is a vibrant Ukrainian community, predominantly living in Melbourne and Sydney.

There are also Ukrainian centres in Geelong, Brisbane, Perth, Adelaide and Canberra. Smaller centres exist in Queanbeyan, Hobart, Newcastle, Moe, Albury-Wodonga, and Northam.

The 1950s saw a huge birth of community organisations, churches and centres.

Ukrainians are proud of their traditions and their 7,000-year-old culture.

Over the years, Ukrainians have built a network of churches, community centres, financial institutions and language schools throughout Australia.

There are Ukrainian studies centres at Monash and Macquarie universities.

Over the decades, Ukrainian Australians have had concerns about the lack of human and political rights in Ukraine — until Ukraine gained its independence on August 24, 1991.

CHAPTER 22
"A DANGEROUS PLACE"

Nurturing her family — in the face of Chile's brutal Pinochet regime and also as new migrants in 1970s Australia — was a life's work for migrant Maria Rodriguez.

One of the defining experiences of Maria's life was standing in front of her students and receiving a 20-minute standing ovation.

The Chilean high school French teacher had recently been released from one of military dictator Augusto Pinochet's prisons. She was locked up for simply supporting his rival Salvador Allende, South America's first ever popularly elected socialist president.

Unlike thousands of others, she survived the experience and managed to escape her troubled homeland and build a new life for her family in Australia.

"It was a moment I will never forget. It was at the end of the year in which I had been jailed and the school where I taught was having a farewell ceremony," Maria said.

"I was presenting diplomas to a group of students I taught all through high school to Year 12. As it came to my turn to hand out the diplomas, everyone stood and applauded. They all knew what had happened to me and they clapped and went on clapping. It was amazing and after everything I had been through, I felt people understood I had done nothing wrong," she said.

Maria says she and her husband were unlikely political activists.

"My husband and I were supporters of Salvador Allende. He was the first socialist president of Chile elected by a popular vote. We volunteered to work for his campaign and we were happy when he won. My family was not politically active but Allende had promised to make a new Chile — to nationalise the wealth of the country especially the copper industry and the banks which were dominated by the US — and we thought it was fantastic, we supported him.

"But the US and the extreme right in Chile were not happy and they plotted to get rid of him and to stop the nationalisation. We thought this would be a phase and that in time things would be OK. And usually after few months a president's popularity declines but it was the opposite with Allende. Even with all the difficulties at the time, the left was doing well electorally."

Maria said that with the help of the Nixon administration in the US, right wing groups in Chile plotted to destabilise the Allende regime. She says they created shortages of food and other necessities and orchestrated strikes.

"They hoped people wouldn't know who was behind this and they would blame the government," she said.

In 1973, three years after Allende's election, a political and constitutional crisis emerged with the Supreme Court and opposition politicians opposing Allende's nationalisation agenda.

In June an army tank unit surrounded the presidential palace but failed to depose the government.

Maria says the failed coup d'etat — which became known as the Tanquetazo or "tank putsch" — was a rehearsal to test popular opposition to the military taking control.

In September, Allende was planning to resolve the crisis with a referendum on his plans. He was due to speak publicly about this but he was not able to because the Chilean military, backed by the US, staged a coup in which Allende was killed.

Coup leader General Agusto Pinochet became Chile's new president.

In the aftermath of the coup, known supporters of Allende were rounded up and almost two-and-a-half thousand simply disappeared.

It was time of fear for many Chileans, including for Maria and her husband Sergio.

"After the coup, people who were supporters of Allende became targets," Maria said.

"My husband was an electrical engineer working for a sugar refinery and he had been active in the trade unions. He was removed from his managerial position."

Maria said that after a time things seemed to return to normal. Sergio had been demoted but he still had a job. She continued to work as a high school French language teacher.

"But we were worried about what might happen in terms of our two daughters and what would become of them in the future," she said.

With this in mind they made enquiries with the Australian embassy in Chile about immigrating to Australia.

At the time the Whitlam government was accepting people who had fallen foul of the Pinochet regime.

"We were told that because we were still working and not in prison we were not eligible and that the Australian government was trying to help people who were in danger," Maria said.

Maria had always held fears for Sergio because of his trade unions links, but in October 1974 it was she who was arrested and jailed.

"The military had a list of people who had supported the previous government and one day they came to my school and arrested four men and myself. We were taken away and our families were not notified. It seemed we had just disappeared."

Sergio desperately tried to find out where Maria had been taken and eventually discovered through family friends who had contacts in the government that she was being held by the navy in a fort in Valparaiso — the port city where they lived.

Maria told of being interrogated by naval officers.

"They asked if I had weapons and who else was in the group supporting Allende. I was there for five days and during that time I saw no one — no family, no lawyers," she said.

At one point Maria was blindfolded and told to sign a statement.

"When I read it I told them 'I didn't say any of this' but I had to sign it. Then one day they came to me and said, 'get your things, you are leaving'. They took me to a women's prison which was full of drug traffickers — it was a very dangerous place. Thank God they had a separate section for political prisoners because I'm sure many of us would not have survived in there. At that time I felt lucky to still be alive because a lot of people disappeared. Politicians, artists disappeared and a lot of people were tortured," she said.

Maria's daughter Pamela says that while her mother was in prison, her father reassured her and her sister Andrea that their mother had been posted to boarding school out of town and that she would come home eventually.

"From Dad's perspective, his wife went to work one day and didn't come home. But he made up this story about where she was to calm us. It is interesting to see some of the things people will do to protect children," Pamela said. "Once when we visited mum at the prison, she had convinced some of the other younger women who were locked up with her to pretend that they were her students."

After a month in prison, Maria was released.

"I went back to work and continued to get my salary but I had to report to the navy headquarters once a week. It was a very bad time for all of us," she said.

Having been a political prisoner, Maria and Sergio made fresh application with the Australian embassy in Santiago and this time they were accepted. In March 1976, the Rodriguez family arrived in Australia.

"It was a very good feeling. We were not scared anymore and the girls were at school and we could see they could have bright futures here," Maria said.

The family lived with friends for a month before moving into a flat in Balaclava. They arrived on a Saturday and the following Monday Sergio was working at the Ford factory in Broadmeadows. He worked in a series of factory jobs before finally landing a role commensurate with his experience at the State Electricity Commission. Sergio died in 2007.

Maria worked the afternoon shift at Westpac in the city for 15 years doing data processing.

"Mum would start work at 1pm and come home at nine so we didn't see much of her during the week. She would pre-cook a meal and we would come home and have dinner with dad," Pamela said.

Both daughters went to university and built successful lives for themselves; Pamela studied social work and Andrea teaching.

"Coming here was good for our kids and for us. Ordinary people were very friendly and helpful. We found peace and tranquillity and here there was no persecution," Maria said.

Maria passed away peacefully on April 7, 2022. She was diagnosed with lung cancer in July 2021 and dealt with her illness courageously. She spent her last few months in her home surrounded by family and loved ones. This gave her much comfort and love.

She is survived by her two daughters and two granddaughters.

CHAPTER 23
JOURNEY OUT OF AFRICA LEADS TO ARARAT

The rocky granite hills and Grevillia scrub around Ararat are a long way from the high grassy plateaus and soaring mountains of Ethiopia. And the sleepy streets of the former gold rush town are a world away from the brutal violence that currently besets much of the Horn of Africa. But one refugee family from the strife-torn African country has found a new home in the quiet western Victorian community.

Each weekday morning Ararsa Wakjira and his two younger brothers would climb aboard their bicycles and ride the five kilometres to their jobs at Ararat's meat processing factory.

At Ararat Meat Exports the brothers are employed in the physically demanding work of butchering and processing meat for export. After up to ten hours of toil, they ride their bikes home again.

"The work is hard but I am strong," says Ethiopian refugee Ararsa.

His words resonate with the painful history of his Ethiopian homeland, a nation which has suffered decades of war, civil conflict, drought and famine.

The interminable conflict in Ethiopia continues today as fighting escalates in the north of the country between the federal government and the Tigray People's Liberation Front.

Ararsa and his brothers Buzayo and Geda moved to the Wimmera town in October 2020 to take up jobs after having spent more than a year struggling to find ongoing work in Melbourne.

They are part of part of a new project which aims to support refugee families find jobs, homes and social and educational networks in regional towns.

The brothers arrived in Australia from Cairo in 2019, where they had sought refuge from conflict and political persecution in their home in the city of Shashamane, in Ethiopia's south, in 2016.

Subsequently, they have been supported to resettle in the town by migrant and refugee settlement agency AMES Australia in partnership with the local chapter of a group called Regional Australians for Refugees (RAR).

"Ararat people are lovely people. They are very friendly and we feel very welcome," Ararsa said. "And the town is good for me because now I have work. In Melbourne it was very difficult to find a job but here is good."

With the help local volunteer groups Rural Australians for Refugees Ararsa and his brothers have bought a car and learned to drive so they no longer have to cycle to work. The brothers share a house where they spend their weekends entertaining local friends and sharing Ethiopian coffee with their visitors. And recently, they have joined a local soccer club with the support of RAR.

Buzayo, 25, says he prefers life in Ararat to being "bored" in Melbourne.

"I enjoy living here. In Melbourne it was hard to get a job but here we are busy and we are better off. We play tennis and we go swimming in the lake," he said. "The people in Ararat are very nice, some of them have become like family to us. We feel very welcome. We have our house and everything we need. Five days a week we work and on Saturday and Sunday we have visitors and we make coffee for them. Now people in Ararat know about Ethiopian coffee and maybe we'll open a coffee shop."

The brothers left Ethiopia at different times and were reunited by the Red Cross as refugees in Cairo. They fled the civil and political unrest in Ethiopia. Buzayo spent three years in Cairo and he says his brothers were there longer.

"There was no peace in my country. We had to leave because of the war and the politics. There was mistreatment of us by the government," he said. "But also in Egypt it was very difficult to live. We could not get jobs.

I worked for a while in a petrol station."

But Buzayo has dreams of starting his own business.

"In Ethiopia I used to have my own truck. In Australia I hope to buy my own truck ad house and drive my truck in my own business," he said.

Their support worker Mirrin Pedro said the brothers were determined to build new lives in Ararat and make the most of the opportunities the town presents.

"They are keen to become part of the local community and they're eager to get drivers licences so they can buy a car and see more of their adopted region," Mirrin said.

She said they were being assisted in this goal by a Rural Australians for Refugees (RAR), which is a network of regional and rural groups supporting and advocating for refugees and people seeking asylum.

RAR member Bonnie Carter says her group was also able to furnish the brothers' house and supply them with the bicycles and helmets.

"They are lovely men and we have been overwhelmed with offers of help to support them to settle in Ararat. They arrived with literally nothing but the local community stepped up to help," Bonnie said. "We have also helped them with dental appointments and connecting them with Telstra. But this support is all aimed at seeing the brothers become independent and able to navigate the local community themselves."

Bonnie was also able to help Ararsa get a second job as a cleaner at a local school. He was keen to earn more money to send home to family members still in Ethiopia.

Ararsa said that the brothers' new lives in Australia now held out the prospect of a bright future.

"Life in Australia makes me very happy. I now have this job and the RAR people have made us feel very welcome. I'm happy in Australia," he said.

CHAPTER 24
ANCIENT QUEEN INSPIRES NEW COMMUNITY

Ancient Syrian queen Zenobia was a cultured monarch who fostered an intellectual environment in her court, opening it to scholars, artists and philosophers. Tolerant and protective of religious minorities, she has become much a loved historical figure across the Middle East.

Zenobia is also the inspiration behind a new support group based in Melbourne's north is helping newly arrived migrant and refugee women navigate their new lives in Australia. The not-for-profit organisation is supporting women, particularly from Arabic-speaking backgrounds establish new lives in a new society.

The group's programs provide advice and information on a range of important aspects of life in Australia including: vaccinations and COVID-19, mental health, Centrelink services, aged care, and the health and education systems.

The women are also volunteering to help vulnerable people in the broader community.

Founder and former Syrian refugee Norma Medawar said that group had been meeting remotely on Zoom late last year but planned to meet in person when the Covid pandemic has abated.

"We have been running a Saturday citizenship program for the women to help them understand how Australian society works and what services are available to them," she said. "We have also been running yoga and meditation classes for the women — some of whom have become anxious and disconnected — sometimes because of having to isolate. So far the classes have been online but we are looking for a venue where we can meet together when that is possible."

She said the group's plans included an art exhibition for women migrants and also fundraising for disadvantaged people in her Syrian homeland.

"We want to do more to help and support migrant women through things that bring people together like food and arts events. We are also encouraging women to do volunteer work to learn more about Australian culture and integrate better in the society. We've already volunteered to help Citylife Church in Lalor through cooking Middle Eastern food for isolated and homeless people. We've done this twice and we are planning to do more," she said.

Norma said the group's philosophy is to be inclusive and to empower women to take full places in society and achieve their social and economic goals. She said it was with this in mind that she came up with the name Zanobia. The third century queen maintained a stable administration which governed a multicultural and multi-ethnic empire. Zenobia died after 274 AD, and many tales have been recorded about her fate. Her rise and fall have inspired historians, artists and novelists, and she is a patriotic symbol in Syria.

The group has also launched a campaign to support the children of families in Syria who are falling into poverty and destitution as a result of a decade of war and the COVID-19 pandemic.

Pandemic restrictions, the collapse of the Syrian economy and the displacement of millions of people have led to an unprecedented number of families in Syria who are no longer able to put food on the table or make enough money to afford basic necessities, aid agencies say.

In response, the Zenobia group along with Melbourne's Syrian community is raising money for a charity based in Damascus that supports the children of families in financial difficulties.

Norma said she and three other Melbourne-based Syrian women

— Caroline Jalhom, Luna Ghawi, Amal Ibrahim ad Narisa Khamisy — formed the support group.

"The plan is to help to families who are struggling to provide for their children," said Ms Medawar. "Kids from all religious backgrounds have suffered as a result of the war and the COVID-19 pandemic has made things even worse."

The group has produced video clips to explain the size and scope of the humanitarian crisis in Syria.

"We want people to know that even though most of our attention is currently focused on the pandemic here, in Syrian there is a massive humanitarian crisis emerging," Norma said.

Aid agencies say staggering 9.3 million Syrians are now going to sleep hungry and more than another two million are at risk of a similar fate — part of an overall rise of 42 percent in the number of Syrians facing food insecurity in the past last year.

Millions of Syrians are now in desperate need of help. According to the UN, $US3.29 billion was required to meet the urgent needs of the most vulnerable Syrians in 2019 — but only about half of that has been received.

Since 2011, over half of Syria's pre-war population — more than 12.7 million people — have been forced to flee their homes due to conflict.

Unemployment is close to 50 per cent, compared with 42 per cent the previous year and food prices are 240 per cent higher than in June 2019, according to the UNHCR.

More than nine million people in Syria are living with food insecurity — with over two million more, at risk of joining them.

Many internally displaced Syrians have sought refuge in Damascus putting added pressure on the city's infrastructure and services.

Norma said things were getting worse for many people in Syria each day.

"We know 2020 was a difficult year for everyone in Australia and we understand if you can't help us right now, you might still be interested in learning a little more about life in Syria today," she said. "We are devastated by the current situation and while Syrians throughout the country are struggling to access the basics."

The group has a personal link to the St Paul's Catholic Church childcare centre in Damascus and know the challenges it is facing to deliver much needed community services.

"We are connected through our friend Caroline who has cherished memories of her childhood spent with the nuns, and her friends at St Paul's. She remains in touch with the nuns to this day," Norma said.

St Paul's Church provides childcare to approximately 150 children aged 3 to 6 years, and more recently mental health programs to 100 children aged between 6 and 13 years. Children of all religions are welcome at the centre.

In Syria, AUD$50 will buy a school bag, shoes, tracksuit and art smock, books, stationery, arts and crafts supplies for one child.

CHAPTER 25
JOURNALISTS CARRY THE TORCH OF FREEDOM

From a small newsroom and studio in suburban Melbourne a group of exiled Burmese journalists are beaming news, interviews, information as well as hope and encouragement back to the people of their beleaguered homeland.

The group of four are part of the Democratic Voice of Burma (DVB), an independent, not-for-profit media organisation and TV channel that has been promoting democracy and human rights in Burma for more than 30 years.

Following the February 2021 military coup, the organisation was banned and some of its reporters locked up for daring to challenge the new regime.

Some DVB journalists have made their way to Australia as refugees and are continuing their work, trying to inform the people of Burma about what is happening in their country and the world despite heavy media censorship by the military.

The group's leader Nay Thwin Nyein was a household name in Burma before the coup.

"Before the coup I worked on DVB's TV debate program as the moderator. It ran on free to air and satellite TV channels with a focus on politics, human rights, social harmony and the peace process," Nay Thwin said. "It was a well-known program, one of the most famous news shows in Burma. We had lots of high-profile people debating about political issues in the country."

But the 2021 military coup in Burma coming after a general election in which Aung San Suu Kyi's National League for Democracy (NLD) party won by a landslide, everything changed.

Amid the brutal crackdown led by coup Leader General Min Aung Hlaing, which saw widespread killing and torture of civilians, DVB was banned.

"When the military took control we didn't know what to do. We knew the military would not allow our content or independent voice," Nay Thwin said.

"A month after the coup, they cancelled out registration and we became an illegal organisation in my country. We couldn't work legally or openly anymore so all our reporters went undercover. And people like me, who were well known, had to go in to hiding. At first I tried to hide in Rangoon, the capital, moving from place to place and staying with friends. At that point there was relative calm and things were peaceful. But a few days later the military showed their true colours and cracked down violently on people opposing them. They killed demonstrators and arrested journalists, including some of my friends. It became too dangerous for me to stay with my friends so I moved to a rural area."

Nay Thwin found refuge in the Kareni State, home to an ethnic minority group that has long been persecuted and targeted by the Burmese military.

"My plan was to find a safe place to continue my work of reporting the truth about what was happening under the protection of the Kareni militia groups," he said. "I was able to stay in a Christian church and tried to continue my work. But there was no internet and only some telephone connections. I tried to report on what was happening but it was difficult."

It was then that Nay Thwin received am message from DVB's head office in Oslo that he should try to get to Thailand to join with other colleagues and try to resume their work.

"Some of my colleagues had joined me in the Kareni state and so together we travelled to Thailand illegally," he said. "We walked overnight for six hours across some rugged mountains. It was exhausting and scary. When we made it into Thailand we were met by friends with a car and we drove to Chang Mai. We changed cars two or three times — I don't really remember because I fell asleep."

Nay Thwin and seven colleagues set up their operation in a house in Chang Mai, producing news content, interviews and debates, mostly delivered online.

"We arrived in Chang Mai just before the Songkran water festival but there were no celebrations because it was during the Covid period. We managed to rent a house and continue our work.

"We were working quietly. We knew we were in Thailand illegally but it was impossible to continue to work in my country so we felt an obligation to try to keep the channel going. We felt we had a duty to let people know what was going on.

"Almost all of the independent media in Burma has been abolished by the regime and they have stopped working. But we felt we couldn't stop and that our people have a right to know the truth about what is happening in our country," Nay Thwin said. "We would receive reports from out undercover reporters in Burma that were smuggled across the border and we would broadcast them back into Burma from Thailand. We were like a news service in exile. It was very challenging for us but people in Burma were still receiving news."

The Chang Mai operation came to an end one morning when the Chang Mai house was raided by Thai police and immigration officials.

The group were arrested and charged with illegal entry into Thailand. A subsequent court appearance saw them sentenced to seven months in prison and fined. They also faced the even more serious prospect of being sent back to Burma and into the hands of the military.

After the sentencing the group was taken to Bangkok where they expected to be incarcerated in one of the city's notorious prisons. But at this point the journey of Nay Thwin and his colleagues took an unexpected turn.

"We spent one night in detention in Bangkok and we were expecting to go to jail but the next morning we were told there was a United Nations person waiting for us outside. The people from the UN said 'you have to have a medical check-up and them we have a form for you to fill out'. When we saw the form, it said 'Australian Government — Immigration and Citizenship'. It was then we realised the Australian Government was trying to help us. This came as a complete surprise. No one had told us this was happening but we felt very relieved. We thought we would spend time in prison.

"The next day and immigration officer arrived at the gate of our cell. He told us to bring all our belongings and outside the detention centre a police car was waiting for us. At the airport, we met two people from the Australian embassy who explained to us what was going on. At that point we were 100 per cent sure we were safe and we were not being returned to Burma. It was a happy moment.

"If we had been deported back to Burma like some other illegal entrants, we would have been in trouble with the regime. But I think our circumstances were different because we were journalists," he said.

Since arriving in Australia in June 2021, Nay Thwin and his colleagues have established a newsroom and studio in Melbourne, broadcasting news reports and interviews into Burma via DVB's satellite TV channel.

They have a small TV studio, a sound desk and computer equipment set up in a nondescript suburban house.

"While people are protesting and fighting to keep the rights they have won over the past 15 years, we feel we have a responsibility to support them," Nay Thwin said.

"People in Burma have got used to having freedoms and rights based on democratic values. The military have taken those rights away so we are fighting back and an open and free media is key to this, along with a values-based civil society. I hope democracy will return to my country and I believe the Burmese people will keep fighting until their rights are returned. In the meantime, it's our responsibility as journalists to keep doing our job providing true information as we did before."

Another of the group working in Melbourne is news anchor Khin Yupar who arrived in Melbourne from Thailand in April 2022. She had to flee her homeland to avoid a roundup of reporters by the military early in 2022.

"I was helped to cross into Thailand by the Karen National Army, which is the military force of the Karen ethnic group," Khin said. "If I had stayed I could not have continued my work and I may have been locked. For me it was important to continue to do this work and to support the fight for freedom in Burma."

Nay Thwin, whose wife joined him in Melbourne a few months after his arrival, has called on the international community to isolate the Burmese military government.

"I would like to see other nations isolate the Burmese military diplomatically, economically and in terms of business. If they are not given space to breathe, they will stop," he said.

Nay Thwin also than ked the Australian Government for its support.

"I want to thank the Australian Government and people for helping us to be able to continue our work; and for bringing Burmese activists and journalists here."

DVB was founded by a science student after the 1988 uprising. It initially operated mostly outside of Burma — based in Oslo and Chang Mai — because of the threat of arrest by the military junta led by General Ne Win.

Since its establishment, DVB has received funding from the Norwegian and Finnish governments. But after the 2010 elections, the first in Burma in 20 years, DVB was able to operate from within Burma.

"Broadcasting our show only became possible after the 2010 election brought some democracy to Burma so we launched the show and it became very successful," Nay Thwin said. "The election brought some openness and democracy and the new president, former general Thein Sein allowed DVB to return. We were legalised and registered as a mainstream media organisation and we began working in Burma. That all changed in February 2021."

CHAPTER 26
YOUNG AFGHAN'S HOPES AND SPIRIT SURVIVE THE TALIBAN

Afghan evacuee Jalal Ahmadzai writes about how hope endures despite the Taliban's seizure of power leaving the dreams of an entire generation in tatters.

Abrupt change, uncertainty and the unknown often strike fear into the hearts of humans. When events take a turn for the worse at a time when one had been planning the complete opposite, it naturally puts one in a state of shock, blurs one's judgement and makes one lose track of events that follow.

The swift collapse of the Afghan government on the 15th of August 2021 made all of that a reality for all the Afghan people. Our worst nightmare came to reality when the capital city of Kabul fell to the Taliban on a grim Sunday afternoon.

Four and a half decades of war and bloodshed has shattered the dreams of three generations. The never-ending war has touched everything and everyone in Afghanistan. The momentary and temporary period of "stability" raised hope in people, only for those hopes to come crashing down in a matter of seconds.

They say there's always light after dark but it seems the sun never rises for the ordinary Afghan men, women and children, who have never been allowed to live in peace and have always been struggling with a war forced upon them by their neighbours and world powers.

War has been a part of our life for a long time now. Dealing with hardships has been part of our daily routine. After nearly 10 years since the government of Dr Najibullah was toppled by the Mujahidden, there was once again a new government in place backed by the international community that showed the promise of a better future ahead. The establishment of various reconstructive projects and the re-opening of schools and universities gave hope to the Afghans that perhaps their country was once again on path towards modernization and competing on an international stage.

When the Islamic Republic of Afghanistan came to power in 2004 after the 2001 intervention of the United States in Afghanistan, the temporary state of stability was once again established. The younger generation of Afghan girls and boys born amidst the war were once again attending schools and universities where they received an education and the anticipation for a brighter future for themselves and their war-torn nation grew inside them. The swift collapse of the Afghan government put an end to those dreams, anticipations and plans.

As a student at the American University of Afghanistan (AUAF), I was lucky enough to be part of the AUAF community, Afghanistan's highest-ranking university that provided world class education to the young generation of Afghanistan. Like me, there were hundreds of students at AUAF and millions of young people across Afghanistan attending various universities all of whom had goals, dreams and objectives that they wanted to reach after graduating. We, the younger generation of Afghanistan, were constantly defying the odds and getting an education amidst the unrest in the country and hoping that one day we would be able to serve our country with the skills we have learnt and secure a promising future for ourselves.

Despite the continuous conflict that raged in different parts of the country, our parents and elders did their best to give us everything they never had. Our generation was raised with dreams and visions of rebuilding our country and bringing a positive change. In the past 20 years, many were able to contribute to this cause and we believed we were going towards a better future. We are children of war but we were never hopeless.

However, now that better future we were always dreaming about lies beyond the bounds of possibility. All that we see now is an endless grey horizon of uncertainty and helplessness. It hurts that we couldn't protect what we had achieved and had to leave them in wrong hands. It wasn't just the fall of a country, but of a whole generation, that had worked itself to rise and were committed to this nation.

Many of us succeeded in escaping the darkest regime, leaving behind our families, friends, and loved ones. Not only that, we left behind our lives, our dreams of graduating and serving our country. We all can continue our lives outside Afghanistan peacefully, but there always be a sadness engraved deep in our hearts. We will be strangers wherever we go and the feeling of being homeless will never leave. I thought we were very close to the better future we believed could exist, but now it feels like someone hit the reset button and we are back at beginning of the tunnel.

I will always remember those last days we spent in Kabul. There was a lot fear and apprehension about what would happen once the Taliban took full control. Thousands of people were desperate to escape the country. My university, which was obviously associated with the United States, told us to get rid of all of the documents we had that could link us to the institution. That meant all of my ID documents, notes, essays — everything I had worked on over four years had to be destroyed.

It was heart-breaking, but I had to get rid of four years of my life. I travelled across the city, through Taliban checkpoints and past groups of militia fighters, to get to the house of a relative where I was able to set fire to all the materials.

It was dangerous and I was concerned that I would be searched and identified as a student of the American University, which could have put my life at risk. Nonetheless I packed everything in a bag and set out.

I watched four years' worth of material burn in front of me and it made me reflect on how much my people have lost over the years. The fire burning in front of me made me think about how much the burning of a few pieces of paper which were already digitalized still engraved sadness in me. It also made me reflect on the pain of millions of other Afghans who have had to let go of bigger things or even people in this long and bloody war.

A few days later, my family and I were able to get into the airport and on a flight out of the country. As the plane took off, I looked down at the dusty, gloomy city that harboured the pain and grief of millions and millions of people over the years and appeared to have no escape route from the group of people that have sworn to destroy its very foundation and roots. Leaving this city in the wrong hands filled me with guilt and I felt as though someone had placed a heavy rock on my chest. So much so that for a minute I felt like I couldn't breathe. I looked around me at the people seated on the plane, the same horrified, uncertain and ambiguous look one everyone's faces as we set out on a one way trip from our home, the Kabul that we all loved.

My mother always said that one's country is like one's mother, and must be treated the same. An Afghan must take care of their country like their own mother, respect it and love it the same. The events of the 15th of August made me understand this concept very deeply.

Yet somewhere deep in the unknown corners of my heart, a rebellious spark of hope lurks, a thing that cannot be quite obliterated. I will always dream of the day I can go back to my home and wander through the streets of Kabul.

CHAPTER 27
A PASSPORT TO THE WORLD

For Burmese migrant Sanda Aye, life has always been a path less travelled.

From working in a fish cannery in Alaska to becoming a fashion consultant for a giant US department store and running a successful international photo library, she has always seized every opportunity and embraced diversity and change.

After fleeing Burma's brutal military dictatorship in the 1970s, immersing herself in Seattle's grunge culture and dropping out for a year in Cairns, Sanda's life reads like a travel classic.

Her CV also extends to managing a fashion retail store, working in international sales and event management in the commercial marine industry and running her own business designing computer backpacks that are made in Victoria, Australia.

More recently, Sanda has been using her experiences of having to flee her homeland to help other refugees as a volunteer in Melbourne.

"I think adaptability and flexibility have been the key to my life. For me travel is joy and I've always travelled as much as I can," Sanda said.

Now semi-retired and living in inner-city Footscray, she volunteers to help newly arrived refugees adapt to their new circumstances.

And, in a circuitous stroke of fate, some of the people she helps also are from Burma.

"I left Burma in 1978. I lived in Malaysia for a year and then migrated to the US where I lived until 1989," Sanda said.

In 1978 Burma was ruled by a brutal military government headed by General Ne Win.

Through the 1970s student-led protests against the government were crushed by the military. In one incident in 1974 thousands of students and workers were shot at a textile factory.

"We left Burma out of political necessity. My parents had fallen into disfavour with the government and the ambassador to Malaysia brokered a deal where my father got a contract to work at a new medical university in Malaysia," she said.

"He was a Professor of Medicine, an FRCP, specialised in Malariology and they needed someone to head the department of medicine in a new medical school. When we got out of Burma we had freedom, it was fantastic," Sanda said.

But like most migrants, Sanda and her family experienced setback and challenges when they left behind all that they had known and loved.

"When we arrived in Kuala Lumpur because of the Malaysian bureaucratic system, my father was not paid for six months and because my parents could not bring any currency out of Burma except US$ 8 per person, we had no money.

"My mother had worked for oil companies in Burma and through these contacts some friends gave us interest free loans. I was just 20-years old and I had just graduated with a BA in English. I had planned to do my masters. However, the Malaysian authorities decided that I was no longer a dependent of my parents and I was given a one-year tourist visa.

"I migrated to the US and went to live in Seattle, Washington, worked for the first two summers in Alaska — in a canning factory, mopping floors and making beds for the fishermen. It was a very strange world but I was paid an obscene amount of money which meant I didn't have to work in the winters that I spent hanging out in Seattle," she said.

Eventually, Sanda got into the fashion industry in the US and ended up working for Seattle-based department store giant Nordstrom.

When her father's contract in Malaysia expired her parents moved to

Hong Kong where her father worked in a hospital.

Unable to return to Burma, they applied for political asylum in Australia and were accepted for settlement in Brisbane.

"My parents moved to Sydney soon after and settled down there," Sanda said.

It was on a trip to Sydney for her sister's wedding that she met her future husband.

"My sister set me up with a French wildlife photographer and we ended up having a long-distance relationship. I would fly across the Pacific for long weekends," Sanda said. "Finally it was easier for me to move to Australia because my husband had a business based here."

She arrived in Sydney in 1989 and worked in fashion for a time before helping her husband run his flourishing photo library.

Her marriage broke up after seven years and she followed her best friend who later became her husband to Cairns.

"After a year in Cairns, we came to Melbourne and we've been here 21 years. Melbourne is the city I have always wanted to live in for its rich culture, music and food scene. And I love the weather — you get sense of the four seasons here," Sanda said.

Recently, Sanda has been volunteering with refugee and migrant settlement agency AMES Australia to support recently arrived refugees. Her ability to speak Burmese means she can make a valuable contribution in helping newly arrived to Australia navigate an unfamiliar society.

"I was looking for something to get involved in and they told me at AMES they needed people who could speak Burmese and English. After my husband passed away, I jumped at the opportunity," Sanda said. "I love volunteering to help people new to this country. I was new here once and I can understand the challenges people have. I am also grateful for the opportunity as the volunteering work has given me tremendous form and structure in reconstructing life after my loss."

She also volunteers with local environmental groups and enjoys canoeing, walking and camping.

"I love the outdoors and the sense of freedom and exhilaration it brings me. I also enjoy contributing to preserve what's left of our natural environment in the city," she said.

Reflecting on the colourful and exciting twists and turns of her life, Sanda said she has no regrets.

"I've truly enjoyed every minute of it and I still am. I would not have had it any other way. Growing up in Burma, we had no freedom. The only time we were issued a passport was when we were leaving the country for good. But I feel lucky that we did leave — it gave me a passport to the world."

CHAPTER 28
TEENAGE REFUGEE A COLLINS STREET CEO

At just 17 Fadi Abo was the founder and CEO of an international cosmetics business with a six-figure turnover.

His online skin and body care company Clarcias sells to clients in more than a dozen countries and has 30 employees.

Just six years after arriving in Australia, having fled the brutal conflict in his Syrian homeland, Fadi has achieved his dream of opening an office on Melbourne's prestigious Collins Street.

"It's just a share office but it lends legitimacy and prestige to the business. For now, it's the culmination of my passion to dive into business and into cosmetics," said the first-year university student, now 19.

Forced to leave their home in Damascus in 2012, Fadi and his family relocated to France where his father Johnny worked as a journalist. They spent time living in New York before finally settling in Australia.

"It was difficult at such a young age to lose everything you ever knew, all your friends, and end up in a whole new world with a different way of thinking," Fadi said.

He said his family became more exposed as the conflict worsened.

"My father was a journalist working for international media, so he was targeted by the government. We also witnessed the escalating violence; there were explosions and a shooting incident at our school during recess one day," Fadi said. "But we are very grateful to be in this beautiful and progressive country. We have been given the resources and opportunity to start a new life. As a result, I have been able to express my love for cosmetics and the business and entrepreneurial side of myself."

He started Clarcias five years ago — selling organic make up, skin care and teeth whitener — and the business has just achieved its third consecutive quarter of growth.

"The COVID-19 pandemic has obviously been tragic but we've had a rush of orders because people are staying at home. We are simplifying the equation for customers with free shipping and a 60-day money back guarantee," Fadi said. "During Covid we did really well, it was a blessing in disguise because people were going online and using the internet for shopping so we had record high orders in 2020."

Like most entrepreneurs, Fadi is an early riser.

"I wake up at 5am daily to maximise and efficiently use my time. I jump straight into work, checking any updates from the company. After a couple of hours of work, I start preparing for university," he said.

"After uni, I head to the gym as I believe fitness is important. Once I am at home I study and finish assignments. Even though I value my company, I want to prioritise my education. After finishing my uni work, I spend the remaining hours of the evening focusing my attention on the company."

He said his passion for business and skincare began when he was a boy who "loved to look and smell good".

His first experience with business came when he used to draw pictures and sell them to his peers around the neighbourhood where he lived in Damascus.

"I also ran an online T-shirt company selling t-shirts with unique designs on them. But now my business is skincare and it's something that I really love doing. I think the business world is very interesting and it has a deep meaning to me."

Fadi's entrepreneurial passion has seen him delve into acting and modelling.

"I think acting is a very important part of performing arts. I think performing and art is very beautiful as you can really transform where a person is going and it can really show someone's emotions and how a person can change their voice and how they can transform into different characters. It's something really interesting and something I want to embody."

Fadi says his plan is to finish his business and law degree at Melbourne University and then continue his business career.

"We are currently transforming the business into more of a distribution operation that is offering more than just cosmetics. Even though I've always known what I want to do, I think university is important. And it is a great experience where you have independence and autonomy. And Melbourne University is really good for me because it's globally connected which is really interesting and good for my work," Fadi said.

His elder brother Akkad is currently studying pharmacy at Monash University.

CHAPTER 29
SUPPORTING REFUGEE ENTREPRENEURS TO "THRIVE"

The adage "from small things big things grow" may have never been more appropriate than when applied to a small micro finance outfit that is doing big things when it comes to supporting refugees to start their own businesses.

More than 170 refugee businesses have received loans from not-for-profit finance provider "Thrive" over the past two years.

Established with the vital financial backing of Westpac, private donors and the generous support of leading companies such as Allianz, Deloitte, Gilbert & Tobin, KPMG, Korn Ferry, LOUD, Newgate and Equifax, Thrive, is registered as a charity with tax-deductible status for donations.

Thrive Chairman Huy Truong said the organisation was created to support refugees and asylum seekers start their own businesses.

"As a result, they create self-employment, become financially independent and integrate faster and more successfully as active contributors to our society and economy," Mr Truong said.

"The economic impact has been significant with the double benefit of reduced welfare payments and taxes being paid. In addition to the economic benefit has been the social benefit that arises with developing a network of customers, suppliers and other local businesses.

"We are able to provide these refugees support because of the generous aid from our strategic partners, volunteers and private donors. Their pro bono and financial support for refugees have enabled Thrive to create a system which lets us assist these entrepreneurs as they navigate through the complex and challenging path of starting, managing and sustaining a business," he said.

"At Thrive, we don't see our clients as asylum seekers and refugees in Australia — we see them as our next entrepreneurs. Because even though they may arrive with just the clothes on their backs, they rarely arrive empty-handed: they bring with them a wealth of experience, skills, innovative ideas and the motivation to build fulfilling lives and livelihoods in a safe country.

"Thrive helps them realise their dreams by providing small business loans and support that enable them to start and grow successful businesses and become financially independent, while actively contributing to Australia's economy and community life," Mr Truong said.

He said the focus of the organisation is on services companies that allow refugees to start working straight away, provided they have the necessary equipment.

"There are certain service segments out there that just lend themselves to people who want to work hard. Things like domestic services like home cleaning, office cleaning, gardening... another one might be things like carpentry and cabinet making.

"Years of experience have shown that refugees who are economically independent, integrate into their new country more quickly. Australia has a burgeoning service-based economy which provides abundant opportunities for self-motivated individuals to start their own business," Mr Truong said.

He said his passion to support refugee entrepreneurs stems from his own family's experience.

As a young boy in 1978, Mr Truong and his family boarded a fishing trawler with 24 others to escape the aftermath of the Vietnam War. The family started a new life in Melbourne.

More than forty years later Mr Truong is now the CEO and co-owner of insurance business ALI Group, Co-founder and Chairman of Thrive

Refugee Enterprise and Member of the Federal Government's Refugee and Migrant Services Advisory Council.

"My father was supporting a war effort with his businesses in southern Vietnam, we were obviously fighting alongside the western forces, Americans and Australians, against the communists and to cut a long story short obviously that didn't work out too well," he said.

"At that time, a lot of my father's peers were being put into re-education camps, so Mum had squirrelled away a bit of housekeeping money, which effectively funded the ticket on a boat to come out to Australia.

"Back then it wasn't quite as developed an industry as it is now, in terms of people smuggling as it were. We came out with fishermen who owned the boat, it was us and four families.

"There were about 29 people on a 10-metre boat, and we made our way through Malaysia, Singapore, down to Indonesia, to try and get across before we arrived in Melbourne. I have largely grown up in Australia.

"After arriving in Australia my father started a business but it failed because it was not capitalised properly. I always thought that if he had been able to get a business loan, it would have succeeded. So I thought it would be a good thing to be able supply seed funding to refugee entrepreneurs when they can't get help from the big banks," Mr Truong said.

Among the entrepreneurs Thrive has supported is Rastegar Fathi who came to Australia from Iran in 2012.

For the first two years, he had no visa and began working as a volunteer for the Salvation Army as a chef, working there throughout 2015.

After moving to Melbourne he opened his first business with a partner. When it opened, Rastegar did not have enough capital to sustain his business.

A friend who had worked with Thrive introduced him to their services and he was provided with pre-loan and post loan support. After receiving the loan, he was able to make his business prosper. Then Rastegar sold his old business and opened up another one with a plan to turn it into a franchise using his brand name "Chubby Chef" Kebab.

With Thrive's help, he has managed to not only grow his business but look towards the future with excitement and pride.

Rastegar has outfitted his entire shop from the bottom up, learning to make his own chairs and even upskilled himself in things like construction and carpentry.

He is a hands-on business owner with the passion for food and learning. His new shop is located in Melbourne on Chapel St, a restaurant district with a diverse and thriving nightlife.

Another loan recipient was Elham Behin Hamgini, who arrived in Australia in 2016 as a refugee.

Elham wanted to find a place in her local community in Sydney and as a result began a course at TAFE for a Diploma in Photography and Photo Imagining.

During her studies, she heard about Thrive and thought it was a great opportunity for her to develop her career. Once she had finished her course she applied for a Thrive Loan to establish her photography business.

She says the process was quick and easy. Thrive provided Elham with information and a volunteer to help her write her business plan, cash flow statements and other necessary documents to start her business.

With Thrive's support, Elham began to understand the basics of running a business in Australia.

"I'm really grateful for all of Thrive's advice and support and I look forward to working with Thrive to further her career in the future," she said.

Another of emerging entrepreneur supported by Thrive is Soheil Ettehadolhagh, who came to Australia from Iran almost four years ago with a dream to work in photography.

His biggest challenges were the language barrier and the new culture he had to adjust to coming from so far away.

He approached Thrive to start his business, UniPic Photography, for help financially and also for business advice.

Thrive was very supportive and quick to respond to any of his queries and gave him the business model he needed to be able to run his business effectively.

Soheil now runs UniPic Photography and his clientele are growing steadily month by month.

Saeed Zarinkob came to Australia from Iran with his young family in 2012. He began his entrepreneurial journey by baking at home for his community.

Within a few short years, he opened up a small bakery in Liverpool, NSW, to continue following his passion.

The biggest difficulties he faced was the language barrier as well as the differences in running a business in Australia compared with Iran. Thrive stepped in and helped Saeed not only financially but also to successfully integrate into the Australian business culture. Thrive helped him get the certification and documents he needed to run his business successfully and happily helped finance the growth of his business.

CHAPTER 30
AMIN'S DREAM — GREENING AFGHANISTAN

Afghan refugee Amin Niazai had a dream to turn the deserts of his country green, creating food resources, jobs and sustainable ecosystems.

Amin, who has a doctorate in Forestry and Biomaterials, developed the plan to transform landscapes ravaged by years of drought and make them productive again while also lifting the living standards of local populations.

But the return of the Taliban meant his dreams remain just that.

"I had a dream and a plan for my country and my studies were all aimed towards this dream of making the deserts of Afghanistan green and to restore the forests of my country," Amin said.

"We had concrete ideas around fighting desertification and reducing the effect of years of drought. This would have improved the lives of people and communities through sustainable forestry and farming initiatives.

"It was a very practical plan to make parts of my country more productive through restoring native species. We have a lot of labour in Afghanistan so there was an opportunity to grow commercial crops such as nuts. But then the Taliban returned and the government collapsed – along with my dreams," he said.

But the 34-year-old has not given up on his dream.

"I still dream that one day we will go back when we have peace and stability and we will rebuild the country," he said.

Almost ironically, since the Taliban came to power last August, Afghanistan has been plunged into a dire humanitarian crisis exacerbated by drought extreme food insecurity.

A recent report from the UN refugee agency UNHCR says people in Afghanistan face one of the world's most rapidly growing humanitarian crises. It says half of the population face acute hunger, over nine million people are displaced and millions of children are out of school.

The document says fundamental rights of women and girls are under attack, farmers and herders are struggling amidst the worst drought in decades, and the national economy is in free fall.

"Without support, tens of thousands of children are at risk of dying from malnutrition as basic health services have collapsed," the report says.

Conflict has subsided, but violence, fear, and deprivation continue to drive Afghans to seek safety and asylum across borders, particularly in Iran and Pakistan.

More than 2.2 million registered refugees and a further four million Afghans with different statuses are hosted in the neighbouring countries, which has stretched the capacity of the neighbouring countries hosting them.

The return of the Taliban has also meant that Amin could not return to his homeland after completing his forestry studies in Japan.

His connection with an Australian development company working in Afghanistan meant that Amin was eligible for a humanitarian visa for Australia and he, his wife and three children arrived last year.

But his extended family remain in Afghanistan where they are vulnerable to Taliban reprisals.

"One of my brothers was an interpreter with Australian troops in Oruzgan province and another was a special forces soldier," Amin said. "We were told by people that we would become targets of the Taliban. My brothers were in hiding and I could not return to Afghanistan from Japan. The Taliban have taken our family car and other things and other family members have been harassed," he said.

Since arriving in Australia, Amin is volunteering with a group called

"Wyntree" at Wyndham, in Melbourne's west, which is establishing a nursery and a "tiny forest". Based on a Japanese model, tiny forests are aimed at restoring small parcels of urban land to their original natural landscapes by replanting native species. The forests restore tree canopies and become localised carbon sinks.

"Using a method invented by a Japanese botanist in the 1970s the forests are dense copses with high biodiversity. They show that plants can thrive in areas the size of a tennis court," Amin said. "The trees in these forests can grow more quickly and absorb more carbon than plantations grown for timber. The local group has no technical expertise but they have an amazing passion for nature and conservation so I am happy to contribute to help them."

Amin has an impressive CV in his field of work, including as a risk mediation and emergency response preparedness officer with the UN's Food and Agriculture Organisation in Afghanistan and as head of a Natural Resources Management Unit funded by US Aid supporting Afghanistan's Ministry of Agriculture.

He also worked with the ministry as a Climate Change and Adaptation Manager and also as a Strategy Implementation Advisor with Australian international development management company GRM International, now known as Palladium.

Amin completed his PhD at the University of Kyoto in Japan.

His research took him to northern Canada, where he developed new methods of determining the extent of environmental change due to drought and the impacts on the long-term growth of ecosystems.

These important studies have helped gain a better understanding of the long-term response of forests to increasing environmental changes.

"We applied a new method to detect growth changes triggered by environmental factors looking at three species of Canadian spruce and poplar trees of various sizes and ages," Amin said. "We took samples from the trees to estimate the annual volume growth of each tree. We saw growth shifts or changes in the phase of volume growth in every tree, and some shift years were common to the plots and species, suggesting the same environmental impact on trees."

Amin says that his priority now is to find a job in his field and support his family.

He has had several interviews and is looking forward to re-establishing his career in forestry research.

"I would like to contribute to the forestry discipline here in Australia. Maybe I can gain some experience and build on my ideas on forestry," Amin said. "Who knows, maybe one day this will help me go back to Afghanistan and realise my dream."

CHAPTER 31
FIGHTING TO SAVE HIS PEOPLE — A ROHINGYA'S STORY

Rohingya refugee Habiburahman fled repression and torture in his homeland and eventually found safety and a new life in Australia.

But he continues to advocate for the hundreds of thousands of his compatriots living in limbo in Bangladeshi refugee camps and countless others struggling under the yoke of Burmese government oppression.

Habib (not his real name) has written a book about his own story and the suffering of his people to draw attention to their plight. Titled *First They Erased Our Name* — it tells of Habib becoming an outlaw in his own country and his subsequent escape. First published in French, he hopes it will bring fresh attention to what he describes as historical prejudices behind the plight of his long-embattled people.

"They are cleansing our people time after time, and then pushing our people from the country. They are demolishing our historical existence," he said.

Habib, now living in regional Victoria, says he also hopes the book preserves the story of the repression of the Rohingyas for future generations of his people.

"There is an ongoing genocide and I can't stay silent. We have to make people aware," he said. "The Burmese Government have repeatedly launched these cleansing actions against my people — they did in 1978 and in 1991. We need the international community to hold them to account."

He said the Rohingyas were demanding four things as part of any internationally broker peace deal.

"We need citizenship granted to our people; we need the restrictions we face on movement, education and employment lifted; we need to be relocated to our original villages, and we need the rehabilitation and reconstruction of our towns," Habib said.

"These four things need to be granted for anything to work. And we need a mechanism for this to be monitored. There are 300 to 400,000 people still living in Burma — half in concentration camps and the other half confined in villages. There are also military commanders that need to be prosecuted. Genocide and war crimes cannot be negotiated away — people have to be held accountable."

Habib was just 21 when he fled Myanmar's Rakhine state and set off on a nine-year journey that would bring him to Australia.

Almost a million Rohingya — a Muslim minority from Buddhist-majority Myanmar — have been forced across the border into Bangladesh in the past two years in the face of an alleged genocide.

Habib says it is just the latest episode in decades of repression and violence carried out against his people by the Burmese Government.

"As a Rohingya, I was oppressed, subject to arrest, forced labour and restriction of movement," he said. "That very persistently exists widely and discrimination and oppression and restriction is institutionalised."

It is two years since the Rohingya were caught in the crosshairs of a Myanmar military campaign in which the armed forces have been accused of mass killings and rapes. The United Nations has labelled the action as "having genocidal intent".

Habib was just three years old when the military leader of his country declared the Rohingya were not one of the 135 recognised ethnic groups that formed the eight "national races".

When he was a young boy he was placed in detention for the first time with his father. He says the institutionalised led to brutal acts committed by those in of authority in Burma.

"The conditions were not even suitable for an animal to live," he said.

"In the prison, there was systematic torture… they have police who will randomly come down and beat you up… they beat me."

He left his homeland in 2000 and spent nine years living precariously in Malaysia.

"At the time I left Burma I was terrified. I had to struggle for my life… struggle to stay alive. I was just thinking that even If I can get one step away… then I will be safe and I will not be put back into prison or torture," Habib said.

He arrived in Australia in 2009 aboard a boat.

"Once we got to Australia, I thought we didn't need to worry for our lives. We had hope of a future. But the feeling changed after I was kept in detention for a long time," Habib said.

He spent 32 months in Australia's immigration detention system, including on Christmas Island. In response to the delay, he staged a hunger strike on the roof of a Darwin detention centre and was convicted of damaging commonwealth property.

Despite being a recognised refugee, he remains stateless today, on a temporary visa with no passport. It has meant he had to turn down an offer to address the European Parliament with his story.

He is one of two million Rohingya now spread across the globe — a diaspora caused by repression and violence that has also seen as many as 40,000 killed in conflict over the past few years.

The Rohingya refugee crisis began in August 2017, following attacks on remote police outposts in northern Myanmar by armed groups alleged to belong to the community. These were followed by systematic counter attacks against the minority, mainly Muslim, Rohingya, which human rights groups have said amounted to ethnic cleansing.

In the weeks that followed, over 700,000 Rohingya — the majority of them children, women and the elderly — fled their homes for safety in Bangladesh, with little more than the clothes on their backs.

Prior to the mass exodus, well over 200,000 Rohingya refugees were sheltering in Bangladesh as a result of earlier displacements from Myanmar.

A 2017 UN report in February this year accused Myanmar security forces of atrocities against the Rohingya that could amount to crimes against humanity.

Animosity between the Muslim Rohingya and majority Buddhist Arakanese people is not a new phenomenon. The origins of the conflict in modern times can be seen as far back as the Second World War, where the Rohingya supported the British rulers, and the Arakanese sided with the invading Japanese forces. Since that time, Burmese history has been littered with conflicts between the two ethnic groups.

Following the country's independence in 1948, both groups faced persecution by oppressive governments, but since then it has been the Rohingya who have been the target of the most violence in the majority Buddhist nation.

In 1978 the Rohingya first encountered their first large scale case of state-sanctioned violence, when the Burmese military forced over 200,000 Rohingya out of the country in a rampant display of killings and rape.

In 1982 the persecution of the Rohingya was legitimised through the passing of the Citizenship Law, which effectively denied citizenship to Burmese Rohingya based on ethnic grounds.

CHAPTER 32
CITIZENSHIP CAPS OFF REFUGEE FAMILY'S JOURNEY

Moved by the images of the body of three-year-old Syrian refugee Alan Kurdi washed up on a Turkish beach in 2014, the then Australia Prime Minister Tony Abbott announced Australia would accept an extra 12,000 refugees from Syrian and Iraq conflicts.

The first of those 12,000 to arrive was Iraqi Osama Butti and his family. They touched down at Melbourne's Tullamarine airport on December 17, 2015.

More than six years on, Osama and his family have become Australian citizens.

"When we came to Australia I felt like we had won the lottery and getting our citizenships feels like we have won the lottery a second time," Osama said this week.

During his family's tortuous flight from their homeland, Osama met the then Minister for Immigration Peter Dutton in Jordan in late 2014 and was handed a visa to come to Australia.

"I thanked Mr Dutton for the opportunity and I thanked the Australian people for offering us a new life in Australia," he said. "I promised him that me and my family would be very good citizens for Australia."

Now as Citizens, Osama, wife Hanan and children Mina and Saif, have become just that.

"My two kids are both studying pharmacy at RMIT and my wife and I are working full time and paying taxes. My wife is a teacher's aide and I am a work broker helping other migrants and refugees find work," Osama said.

He said that he and his family had always felt welcome in Australia.

"From the moment we arrived we were received and welcomed by AMES Australia at the airport and they supported us through that early time. I began to volunteer at AMES and then worked casually as a community guide. Then I got the opportunity to work full-time as a work broker helping other migrants and refugees find employment," he said.

Osama and his family have been in Australia for nearly seven years now.

"During this time as a family we have built a new life in a new country. There were some difficulties to begin with, especially for the kids in completing their studies; they had to cope with a completely different education system," he said. "And my wife and I struggled to find jobs at first but these things mean nothing compared to the opportunities we have enjoyed in coming to this country."

Osama has a master's degree and worked in marketing and commerce in Iraq. But in Australia he embarked on a career in community development and supporting migrants and refugees arriving in his wake.

"I studied for a certificate in community services and I now work as a work broker. My job is to support refugees and migrants find their pathways in Australia, just as we did," he said.

Osama says his family now feel settled in Australia.

"We still have cousins and friends in Iraq but now Australia is our second mother country. It's our home. Australia has given us a lot and we feel like we want to give back. We feel we welcome and that we belong here now. After escaping the conflict in Iraq we are living normal lives and we are trying to contribute to the community," he said.

Part of that contribution was being part of a series on in-language videos filmed last year that explained the workings of the Victorian Parliament.

Osama spoke to the cameras in Arabic to explain what happens in parliament. He told how the Spring Street building is where Victoria's laws are made and where our elected representatives debate issues of importance to all Victorians.

He tells a story about how three days after arriving in Australia, Osama went for a walk around the neighbourhood where he was staying with his sister in Melbourne's northern suburbs.

"Three neighbours — Australians — came out and welcomed me. They understood I was a refugee and where I was from, I'm not sure how. But they said 'do not hesitate' if I needed something to go and ask them. That made me feel very welcome," Osama said.

He says the incident is emblematic of the welcome he, his wife and two children have received as part of the advance guard of the 12,000 refugees from the Syria/Iraq conflict that the then Federal Government promised to settle in Australia.

He says he immediately felt at ease in Australia and was overcome with a sense of relief.

"The thing that first struck me when I arrived in Australia was the order. In the airport when we arrived I could see everything was organised well, there were signs telling you where to go. There are rules and regulations in Australia and people respect them. I knew that Australia would be the new home of my family and a place where they can build their futures and where their dreams can come true. The way of life in Australia reminds me of how we lived in Iraq in the late 1970s and early '80s, everything was calm and safe and the future was clear," he said.

Osama said that life became intolerable for him and his family. As Christians, they were the target of threats by extremists.

"After the dramatic circumstances when ISIS entered my country, a lot of things came to the surface. There was a fear among a lot of people in my country, especially the Christians, of what would happen," he said.

"Even though ISIS did not attack us personally, a lot of things did happen, especially at school with my children. Their friends and classmates started to tell them ISIS would come and kill all the Christians, things like that. Also, because of my work with international companies,

I was very afraid. If I remained in my country, I would have been a target."

He said, at the time, he felt very depressed and pessimistic about the future.

"I was not afraid for my life, I was afraid for my wife and children. When you are forced to stay in an area that is not stable, not safe and in very difficult circumstances, you don't know when you are going to die. Frankly speaking, when I went out in the morning in my country, I never knew whether I was going to come back or not, from bombs, from militia attacks."

Osama said it was an emotional wrench to leave his homeland but he had no option. The family sought temporary refuge in Jordan before being granted a humanitarian visa.

"It is very difficult when you are 50 years old to leave a country where you were born and where you were educated and everything; to leave behind memories, good memories, happy and sad memories. It is hard to leave a place that has been your home," he said.

"It's very difficult for me to change at this age but according to my experience and the things I have seen here, the feeling and the services here, I can say I will have a good life here.

"The golden period of Iraq was the 1970s. After that we had the Iran-Iraq War, then the Gulf War. All of my youth years, 35 years, were spent in my country with war and unstable circumstances," Osama said.

He says he and his family have "won the lottery in being resettled in Australia".

"I already told the Minister of Immigration (Peter Dutton) in Amman that I'm feeling that we are very lucky in being one of the first four families to come to Australia. I don't have dreams or nightmares because when I came here, for the first two or three days, I really slept well because in my homeland sleeping was something difficult for me.

"It's very important to me to know my family is safe. It means a lot because when you feel your family is safe and the future is secure; that is the most important thing a father needs from life," he said.

Osama said that he would like to encourage other refugees settled in Australia to make the most of their good fortune and try to contribute.

"My message is that they are really lucky if they come to Australia because life here is bright and the opportunities to work are great," he said.

"I would say to them: 'in order to let the government have the ability to bring more refugees from your country, you need to work and pay taxes — you need to contribute. Otherwise, maybe other families will not get to come here and have the chance to live here in safety'," Osama said.

And he thanked Australia for giving his family a chance at a new life.

"On behalf of my family I would like to thank the people of Australia and the government for giving me this opportunity to live in this beautiful country. It means a lot for me and my family to consider Australia as a new home for us."

CHAPTER 33
RURAL VOLUNTEERS MAKING A DIFFERENCE IN REFUGEE LIVES

In country towns across Australia groups of quiet achieving volunteers are making a huge difference in the lives of refugee families.

Rural Australians for Refugees is an informal network of regional and rural groups supporting and advocating for refugees and people seeking asylum.

In the flat, sun-bleached western districts of Victoria, one of these groups has helped welcome African refugee families who have found employment, educational opportunities and connections into the local community.

Bonnie Carter helped to found the RAR group in Ararat, formally known as Grampians/Gariwerd RAR, after becoming concerned about levels of support from refugees and asylum seekers.

Since then the group has partnered with migrant and refugee settlement agency AMES Australia to support settling refugee families.

"Through AMES Australia we've worked with families settling in town. The first family was a husband who came first and worked for six months in the abattoir before his family came up from Melbourne," Bonnie said.

"He wanted to get his kids out of Melbourne because they were starting to get into trouble. At the time housing was a problem. It was during the pandemic and the move was difficult. We needed three or four bedrooms for Mary and her kids and that would have been expensive. Some of our RAR members are also members of the Uniting Church and they suggested to do up the old Manse next to the church for the family."

Uniting Church Council members poured in their time and energy fixing up the house to get it to a state that it could be lived in and rented. The put in new carpets and flooring, painted the house and exterior and did a huge tidy up.

"RAR furnished the house through members' donations," Bonnie said.

The next family supported by Bonnie and her group were three brothers from Ethiopia.

"We had an incredible response and we furnished their house as well as supplying kitchenware, linen and everything else they needed to stay in the town. Also, one of our volunteers Paul Ruthven literally gave up hundreds of hours to make sure the brothers could get their driving licenses."

The three brothers were also keen to start playing soccer and the RAR volunteers connected them with a local club and helped them acquire boots and equipment.

Bonnie said the episode prompted the group to set up a "sport support" fund to help new arrivals to join local community groups.

"The boys needed to establish friendship with people their age and others needed to be connected to community groups, so we saw a need and we held a one-off fund-raiser and established the fund to support these refugee families to join community groups — be it sport, or art or something else. The boys now have boots and a soccer ball and have started training," she said.

The RAR group also makes regular cash donations to the Asylum Seeker Resource Centre in Melbourne as well as donations of food, nappies and other goods.

Bonnie says she helped found the group about seven years ago partly as a way of making contribution to what she sees as a major global issue — that of human displacement.

"I heard about a program called 'a home among the gum trees' in which people in rural areas hosted refugees from the city for a weekend. I put an ad in the paper calling for volunteers and six people replied; and that was the start of my work supporting refugees," she said.

As a result, Bonnie was contacted by a man named Terry White who ran a Rural Australians for Refugees group in nearby Maryborough.

"Terry said there was a lack of action in the Wannon electorate which covers Stawell and Ararat. He said he wanted to start an RAR group in Ararat because a survey he had seen suggested there was significant number of people in the town who would be interested. So we organised an event in the Town Hall where we invited (lawyer, author and human rights activist) Julian Burnside to speak. We had 150 people attend and we asked them for a donation and their contact details. From that we got a list of people interested in forming an RAR group and we held out first meeting in November 2014. Now we have about 100 people on our email contact list. About a third are active and we can call on the rest when we need them," she said.

Bonnie says volunteering to support refugees has given her great experiences and has widened her view of the world.

"I've met some really nice people and the whole thing has boosted my faith in humanity. I've met lovely people I didn't know were out there. It's also given me the opportunity to do something meaningful and, you know, kindness goes a long way," she said. "But really it's been wonderful to meet people from other parts of the world. These are good people who can contribute to our community. And meeting them has widened my view of the world. And if you can help people, I don't know why you wouldn't do it."

She says rural people can take a while to warm to people who appear different.

"In small communities people can be insular and wary of strangers but having the families in town is starting to change attitudes slowly. And I think having the kids of refugee families in school is where change will happen. Seeing foreign faces around town is becoming the norm and people are realising the newcomers are not causing trouble," she said.

Bonnie says Mary has joined the local Uniting Church.

"So we've seen them welcomed by church members and coincidentally the church has recruited a new Sudanese minister who starts in August. The communities are preparing a welcome with on his first day at the church, which will be lovely."

Bonnie's RAR colleague Rose Rowe became involved with RAR indirectly through her work as a teacher at Ararat's Marian College.

"I was part of the Justice and Democracy Group at the school, which was founded by the Brigidine Sisters, and through that I got to know about the Brigidine Asylum Seeker Project," Rose said. "Refugees were high up on our list of issues in the group so it was a natural segue, but living rurally makes it hard to offer much concrete support. So when I retired and I found out about RAR it was a chance to team up with some like-minded people."

As part of her volunteering role, Rose supported one of the Ethiopian bothers to get a second job as a cleaner at her former school.

"He was keen to make extra money above his job at the local abattoir so I helped him with an introduction to the school. I helped him with the interview and he got and has been able to maintain the job, which is fabulous," Rose said.

"Also, I have never taught English a second language but I thought I could help out in the sessions that are run each week for our new arrivals. So I support our English teacher. The students are so enthusiastic, they hang off every word and they so much want to better their English. It's lovely to be able to help them. We meet in their homes and they are all big on hospitality so we get to taste Ethiopian coffee. They are so grateful and just want to repay what we are doing for them. Supporting them is just so rewarding for me. It's a wonderful program to be part of and I've learnt a lot about different people and cultures."

The current President of the Grampians/Gariwerd RAR is Leonie Foster.

"The families we have helped are grateful for what has been done to help them settle," Leonie said. "It's been lovely that the experience of coming to Ararat has been mostly positive for these families."

Leonie says that the newcomers have been widely accepted by the community.

"We had one particularly family where everything that went to furnish and equip their home was donated by RARA and the broader community," Leonie said.

Community Engagement Coordinator Mirrin Pedro has worked closely with RAR providing guidance and support to help them understand how they can best channel their enthusiasm and efforts to support the families.

Mirrin said that RAR members had also had the opportunity to upskill through other training programs to build capacity in their group.

"Bonnie, Rose, Leonie and supporters of RAR have done an amazing job. They've done a lot of the heavy lifting in making the settlement of these families a success," Mirrin said. "They have done a lot of fundraising, they've provided wrap around support, drop-ins, food and they've helped families enroll kids in school and get to medical appointments. It's been a big achievement for them to pull all this together. The volunteers have appreciated the opportunity to upskill and to support the settling families from a strengths-based approach, using the families own skills and resilience to continue their settlement journeys."

CHAPTER 34
REFUGEE JOINED THE FIGHT AGAINST THE COVID-19 PANDEMIC

As a 17-year-old Iranian refugee Ghanieh Daghagheleh made a dangerous boat journey seeking safety.

After years of struggle, she and her family have built a new life in Australia. And, in 2020, at the height of the deadly COVID-19 pandemic, Ghanieh stepped up as a frontline worker in the fight against the disease.

As a third-year student in Midwifery and Nursing at Victoria University she applied for and was offered a job as a Health Assistance in Nursing (HAN) at the Royal Melbourne Hospital. She was one of the undergraduate student nurses who were co-opted into the health system to battle the pandemic.

"I am enjoying and feel privileged in getting to work in contributing to the efforts to help beat the virus," said Ghanieh, who is working on critical and acute care wards at the hospital. "It is challenging but very interesting work. I am learning a lot and everyone at RMH is very friendly and supportive," she said.

Ghanieh and her family spent six weeks in detention in Christmas Island and then in Darwin before being released and making their way to Melbourne in 2013.

Her first few years in Australia were tough; being on a bridging visa, she was unable to study or work.

"It was very challenging. The only way I could study at university was to get a scholarship. I applied for a scholarship after finishing year 12, there were 200 applications and only one could be selected. Unfortunately, I wasn't successful," Ghanieh said.

Not deterred, she enrolled in TAFE and studied for a Certificate IV in Health Science Foundations and after six month started a Diploma in Nursing. Eventually, thanks to a scholarship, Ghanieh was able to get into a higher degree course in Midwifery and Nursing at Victoria University in 2018.

"I have always had a passion to study and work in the health care field and thanks to the scholarship, I was able to achieve my dream. However, it was very challenging pathway" she said. "I had three interviews and had to go before a panel. When I got the phone call after a week to say I had been accepted, I didn't believe it and I started to cry. This moment was the key start in achieving my dreams."

The single mum was already working in health care with Ambulance Victoria as an Ambulance Community Officer in Beaufort. Ghanieh is one of six graduates from Ambulance Victoria and Life Saving Victoria's first joint multicultural employment pathways program.

The program trains young people from culturally and linguistically diverse backgrounds to work as ambulance officers in regional communities where caseloads are low and not staffed round-the-clock.

"Beaufort is a beautiful place and I love working in the community. People are different — it's a smaller community and easier to connect with people. My goal is to help the community and give back," she said.

Ghanieh's personal experiences have fuelled the 25-year-old's determination to help others and share her story.

She has worked as a lifeguard with Life Saving Victoria and is a member of the Hope Co-op, an organisation that supports students from refugee backgrounds, and she is a student ambassador at Victoria University.

When the opportunity came to work as a HAN to help fight the COVID-19 pandemic, Ghanieh jumped at the chance.

"When I am working to help people who are ill or distressed, it doesn't feel like work. I feel like this is where I belong, it's my second home. I am ready to do whatever I can to help fight this terrible pandemic. Nothing is more valuable than human life," she said.

Ghanieh and her family are among tens of thousands of Iranians who have fled the country to escape repressive laws and religious mandates or the persecution of ethnic minorities.

More recently, deteriorating economic conditions caused by government mismanagement, the COVID-19 pandemic, and US sanctions have increased poverty and reduced living standards for millions of Iranians.

The NGO Human Rights Watch says the Iranian government has mismanaged and politicised its response to the pandemic, especially its national vaccine procurement plan that was slow and lacking transparency during the first months of 2021.

Human rights activists and anti-government protesters have been arrested in large numbers. Security forces have responded brutally to widespread protests stemming largely from economic issues, including by shooting protesters.

Criminal prosecutions and imprisonment are also being used as tools to silence the voices of prominent dissidents and human rights defenders. Iran's new population law also further limits women's rights to sexual and reproductive health and puts women's health and lives at risk.

Iran's Guardian Council has approved the "rejuvenation of the population and support of family" bill, which outlaws sterilisation and free distribution of contraceptives in the public health care system unless a pregnancy threatens a woman's health.

CHAPTER 35
REFUGEE'S HOPE BURNS ETERNAL, INSPIRES OTHERS

Gomis Rugamba Bakhambu says he is a lucky boy.

Despite surviving the worst genocide in modern history, two decades in a refugee camp and a precarious education that saw him walk 24 kilometres a day to attend school, the Congolese refugee considers himself blessed.

"I would consider myself a very fortunate person. When I tell people my story, they often think that I am the most unfortunate child of Congo, but I am not," Gomis said.

Gomis was just three months old when his family fled their home in the West African nation.

As ethnic Tutsi's they had become the target of militias from the rival Hutu tribe in the aftermath of the civil war and genocide in neighbouring Rwanda.

Gomis' family fled ended up in a refugee camp in Rwanda where they spent the next 22 years.

During the Rwandan genocide of 1994, members of the Hutu ethnic majority in the east-central African nation of Rwanda murdered as many as 800,000 people, mostly of the Tutsi minority.

Begun by Hutu nationalists in the capital of Kigali, the genocide spread throughout the country with shocking speed and brutality.

Ordinary people were incited to take up arms against their neighbours and by the time the Tutsi-led Rwandese Patriotic Front gained control of the country through a military offensive in early July, hundreds of thousands of Rwandans were dead.

Gomis said that many of the Hutus fled to the Congo after the conflict in Rwanda.

"They came and started to attack the rival tribes. They started killing us and took our property and they burned out homes. Many of us fled to Rwanda, Uganda and Burundi. Growing up in the camp, we were very young and we didn't know anything else," he said.

"We played together as children but sometimes we were unhappy because there was not much food and no medicine. Often we couldn't afford our basic needs. But otherwise it was kind of normal; we went to school outdoors under the trees.

"The Gihembe refugee camp became my home together with hundreds of refuge children. Life was good as I knew it and we were not really aware of the conflict as long as we were able to play and have some meals. School was at the camp under the trees and if we were fortunate enough, we were in a classroom with 80 other students in one class.

"I recall, one hot summer day, some of my classmates had to stop school as the food ration was getting smaller and smaller and trying to learn in a hot and crowded classroom with very few resources and a hungry stomach was not easy," he said.

To attend secondary school Gomis had to walk a 24-kilometre round trip.

"As I reached secondary school, the conflict between the two tribes became even worse and with the advent of mass media I saw the tragedy that surrounded my new-found country. I was lucky that the camp had provided us a safe haven, despite its dire condition and we teenagers made the most of our experiences in the camp. Secondary school was no longer offered at the camp and we had to walk twelve kilometres each way, each day to get to school. I would wake at 4am to get to school by 6am for pre-school study. The school day would begin at 8am and end at 2.30pm. We would walk home by 4pm and sometimes there would be no food when we got there," he said.

In 2014 Gomis graduated from high school and was one of just two students in a camp of 17,000 people who won scholarships to attend university.

"Going to university would have been impossible for me until he UNHCR in partnership with the Albert Einstein German Academic Refugee Initiative offered me a university scholarship with the prestigious Mt Kenya University in Kigali. I was again a very lucky boy!

"Throughout my university studies, I made it my mission to use social media to bring hope, friendship and love in a country that was torn by civil war and tribal factions.

"I truly believe that change will happen if young people are enabled to see hope and trust in the future and to reclaim their lives back. I'm sure my classmates and I have made a difference, however small, in how young Rwandans see themselves as opposed to how their parents saw each other during the genocide," Gomis said.

While it was his dream to attend university in the capital Kigali, his problems weren't over.

"Sometimes we were discriminated against in the city. We were told 'you are just refugees'," Gomis said. "It was horrible, as if some people didn't consider us as human. But we had to keep pushing. My only choice was to work hard, study hard and maybe tomorrow will be better. We were Tutsis but from another country, not Rwanda. So we had to work very hard and be very careful.

"At uni, my closest friends were other refugees; they were the only ones who knew I was a refugee. We all we tried to hide the fact because the locals discriminated against us," he said.

In 2018, Gomis completed a Bachelor Degree in Mass Media and Communication and started working with UNHCR as a freelance humanitarian photographer.

Shortly after that, his family's application for humanitarian visa was granted and they moved to Adelaide where they are starting to build a new life in Australia.

"Now I'm studying a Master's Degree in Screen and Media Production at Flinders University and working as a photographer part time," Gomis said.

"I consider myself to be the luckiest boy in the world because of the many opportunities that were given to me and for the many people who inspired me to have hope and to believe in the goodness of humanity in the midst of anger, hunger and pain," he said.

While life in Australia has its challenges, Gomis is optimistic about the future. He has worked with UNHCR in Australia as well in fundraising.

"There are great opportunities in this country and I want to be a visual artist in filmmaking and photography," he said. "I want to explain the real world to people through my images and tell the stories of refugees and humanity across all communities. And I want to work with humanitarian agencies to help those in need; to give back and let other people benefit from the help I got when I was in their situation. Even in Australia, I will continue to inspire my friends who are left in Rwanda to never lose hope and to believe that tomorrow can be better."

CHAPTER 36
FROM ISIS TO COVID — REFUGEE FAMILY'S JOURNEY

After fleeing brutal Islamist ISIS fighters in Iraq and spending six years in limbo as displaced refugees, the first thing Revan Jirajees and her family faced on arrival in Australia was two weeks in quarantine.

Rivan, her husband Rafi Matloob and their three-year-old son Yusef, arrived in Melbourne in 2020, just days after the March 15 COVID-19 pandemic curfew was implemented.

But the ordeal of being cooped up for two weeks was nothing compared to the turmoil they experienced when forced to flee their home in the face of attacks by the terror group ISIS.

Even as the COVID-19 pandemic invaded every sphere of life, Revan and her family were grateful and happy to have reached Australia and safety.

"The fourteen days of isolation was difficult. We weren't expecting it and we didn't know it would happen when we arrived but we managed to get through it. Of course we understood that we had to isolate for our own benefit and for everyone's benefit. The isolation was not just for ourselves but for the safety of everyone," she said.

The family settled into a routine to help pass the time.

"After breakfast we did some exercise and then watched some cartoons with Yusef. Then we would prepare lunch and have an afternoon sleep," Revan said. "After that we would watch some TV and then play in the back garden with Yusef. But now that is behind us, we have settled and we are looking forward to the future," she said.

It was very early one morning in June 2014 when Revan and her family were forced to flee their home in a village near Mosul, in northern Iraq, as the brutal militant group ISIS attacked.

"It was three o'clock in the morning and we were told the army had left and ISIS was coming. The whole village took what they could from their homes and left," Revan said. "ISIS came and destroyed everything. They burned our village and took our belongings. We were left with nothing."

Revan and Rafi had been married just six months when they, along with most their village, fled — finding refuge in the Kurdish-controlled city of Irbil, to the west.

They stayed with Rafi's uncle for a month and then moved into a camp near Irbil arranged by their Assyrian Christian Church with up to three families living in small houses.

Finding work was difficult in Irbil because the couple spoke no Kurdish. For a time Revan worked as a front office manager using her English skills and Rafi found some work as an engineer. During this time, Yusef was born.

But when the church organisation ran out of money, the family was left with the choice of either going back to their village and trying to rebuild their lives or leaving Iraq.

"In our village, everything was gone. There was no money, there was no work. And there was no peace, the security situation was very bad. So we decided to leave Iraq," Revan said.

Early in 2019, the family moved to Lebanon. And in March 2020, they arrived in Australia as refugees sponsored by Rafi's sister who had lived in Melbourne for several years.

"We didn't know a lot about life in Australia and at first it was hard because we couldn't go out. But we were very keen to learn, to improve our English and to start out lives in Australia," Revan said.

She said she feared for her family still in Iraq and her brother in Lebanon, whom she wants to bring to Australia.

Rafi's family are scattered across the globe. His parents are in the US, he has a brother in Germany, two sisters in the Czech Republic and a sister here in Australia.

The couple say that, like everyone, they were concerned about the COVID-19 pandemic but feel lucky to be in Australia.

"The pandemic was scary, sure, but there was nothing we could do? And Australia seemed to cope with it well; it has turned out well for most people and we are all OK," Revan said. "This supports how we felt from the start — from the first time we arrived here in Australia — we felt like it was our new country. People have been kind and there is lots of support. Everyone is equal here and there are no religious differences like in Iraq."

The family have settled in Craigieburn, in Melbourne's north, and are getting on with life.

Rafi works as forklift driver with a company making caravans and Revan is studying for a Diploma in Community Service while also volunteering with the Salvation Army.

"Life is good for us. We are moving on with our lives and we have big ambitions," Revan said. "I am studying to improve myself and get ahead. I'm also volunteering with the Salvation Army as a receptionist and also with translating for case managers with Arabic speakers. The work is interesting and I hope the experience will help me get a job. Yusef is in kinder and doing really well. We are very happy and grateful to be here and we feel like we have given Yusef a future."

CHAPTER 37
AFGHAN FAMILY'S INCREDIBLE JOURNEY CELEBRATED IN EMOTIONAL REUNION

Afghani woman "Amina" is an unlikely superhero.

The diminutive, bespectacled Hazara woman brought her three children out of Afghanistan and to safety in Australia despite not having complete visas documents and while being on a Taliban hit list.

As the Taliban took full control of the beleaguered nation on August 15, Amina and her three children navigated their way through a series of militant checkpoints and made it to Kabul's international airport.

There, they braved suicide bombing attacks, tear gas and human stampedes to make it into the safety of the airport terminal.

With documents showing her husband "Baqir" was living in Australia as a citizen, she was able to get her family onto a military flight to freedom.

Her story's happy denouement came two weeks ago when Amina, her son Hussain and two daughters were reunited in emotional scenes in Melbourne with their husband and father after 12 years apart.

Baqir had fled an earlier iteration of Taliban persecution more than a decade previously.

Amina and her family recounted their incredible journey to safety and freedom in the hope that it will for help to prompt the international community do more to help the people of Afghanistan, now facing a repressive Taliban regime as well an economic meltdown and drought amounting to a growing humanitarian crisis.

Their names have been changed to protect their identities over safety concerns for loved ones still in Afghanistan.

"My husband had been in Australia for 12 years — we had met only a couple of time in Pakistan over those years," she said.

"It was very difficult to be separated from him and the situation in Kabul had become unpredictable and very dangerous.

"It was very disheartening and difficult when the Taliban took over; everything fell apart very quickly. Everything we had hoped and dream of vanished. The Taliban were going door to door looking for people who had worked for western governments or military; and people with ties overseas."

Amina was one of the people in danger as an effectively single mother with a husband overseas. But luckily she had no contact with the Taliban.

"When the Taliban took over we were very worried. Our application to come to Australia was being processed so we called my husband but there was no update," she said.

"We decided we had to leave the country so we went to the airport. It was difficult to get to the point where we could enter the airport. There was the risk of suicide bombings and the stampeding crowds around the airport — there were a lot of people there.

"I had never seen or experienced anything like this. But we risked out lives to get to the airport and then we were very lucky that our documents, which were not complete, were accepted and we were allowed in.

"We had no option but to leave no matter how difficult it was. Life under the Taliban was impossible for us. As a woman I had no rights, I could not even go out shopping or do anything.

"With my husband overseas and not with me, it was difficult as the Taliban were looking for people like me. I was very worried and very scared but I knew I had to get my family to safety."

Son Hussain (19) said his school came under threat from the Taliban at times.

"Many times we were told not to go to school. Most of the students were Hazara so it was a target and also it taught English. I was learning English because I was hoping to go to Australia," Hussain said.

Hussain says he and his two sisters are desperate to get back to school.

"My sisters and I want to study and get an education and then get jobs and become useful additions to society. That's our aim."

Amina and Baqir said they were grateful to have found a safe haven in Australia for their kids. And they are keen to see their children get and good education and contribute to Australian society.

"It was very difficult to be apart from my husband but now we are very happy and grateful to be reunite with him here in Australia," Amina said. "I want to thank the Australian government and people for supporting us as we get on our feet here in Australia."

Baqir has been working as a tiler in Melbourne's south east.

He arrived in Australia in 2011 and is now a citizen. He made to his way to Indonesia and came to Australia by boat.

"I left because of the Taliban and the security situation. I was only able to see my family a couple of times in 12 years. We met in Pakistan," Baqir said.

"Those with family members abroad are harassed by the Taliban. They knew I was in Australia and sometimes they would come in the night and my wife was beaten. My family left for the airport with no visas. They were lucky to get on a plane. Amina showed the documents she had with her that said I was here in Australia and they allowed my family through. It was a very big risk they took and I'm happy they got out and did not get killed. It is amazing they are all still in one piece."

Baqir said he didn't know of his family's bid for freedom.

"I was at work when they left. They called me from the airport. They said 'we are at the airport with the Australians'. I could not believe it. I was very worried because I could not help them in any way because everything happened so quickly. I last saw them in Pakistan four years ago. This is unbelievable for us. I am very happy and very lucky they are here with me."

Baqir says he sees a bright future for his family.

"I have been away from my family for 12 years and now we are reunited and will remain so and build a new life together. I want my kids to get an education and do what they want. Maybe become doctors or lawyers or engineers and make valuable contributions to Australia."

CHAPTER 38
BURUNDIAN REFUGEE RISES ABOVE WAR, DISABILITY TO FIND A NEW LIFE

The broad sunlit fruit blocks and paddocks of Mildura are a world away from forested hills of Burundi. But for one Burundian refugee, life in the Victorian city is offering the chance to rebuild a way of life lost in the turmoil and violence of his homeland's interminable civil strife.

Jean Claude Nsabimana was shot in both legs by a gang of armed thugs who also shot and killed his younger brother when his family became the victims of ethnic-based sectarian violence.

Jean Claude says he had a good life working as a bus driver and taxi owner in his East African homeland before the conflict broke out. But the war cost him his home, his job and very nearly his life — and left him with a disability.

After fleeing with his family, he endured more than four years of precarious life in refugee camps in Rwanda and Kenya before being resettled in Australia.

Ethnic tensions have been bubbling under the surface in Burundi, one of the poorest countries in the world, as a result of the civil war that caused the deaths of more than 300,000 people between 1993 and 2005.

Violence between Hutu groups and the minority Tutsis flared again in April 2015 when President Pierre Nkurunziza announced he would seek an unconstitutional third term in office.

A failed army coup in May saw hundreds killed and tens of thousands more flee the country. Jean Claude was caught up in the turbulence.

"My problems started in 2015. Because I am an ethnic Tutsi, I was targeted," Jean Claude said. "I had been in a relationship with a women from the Hutu ethnic group and we had a daughter together. Because of the relationship a group of Hutu men came and asked me to join their group. When I refused, my problems started and I had many troubles. These men insisted that I join them and I continued to refuse. One day the men came to my family house and attacked us. They shot dead my younger brother and they shot me in the legs. When we were attacked, our neighbours came to help us and the gunmen left. My wife Dancila contacted the Red Cross and I was taken to hospital. I had surgery but the doctors could only fix one of my legs."

Jean Claude said that while in hospital, he continued to be a target for the gunmen.

"While I was in hospital, the same group came to attack me. They tried to kill me in hospital, to finish me off. After that, the Red Cross came and heard my problem and took me to Rwanda. At first I was in hospital. I had more surgery but my leg could not be saved and it was amputated. UNHCR paid all my medical bills and eventually took me to a refugee camp in Rwanda. I stayed there for two and half years with my wife and kids. But while I was in the camp, a lot of people from Burundi came and I was harassed again."

Jean Claude and his family were moved to the giant Kakuma refugee camp in Kenya, one of the world's largest, which is currently home to more than 190,000 displaced people.

"We were at Kakuma for two years. Life was not easy. I was disabled and it was difficult to do much," Jean Claude said.

With Jean Claude safe from Hutu retribution, the gangs turned their attention to his mother and father.

"Because they couldn't get to me, the Hutu groups attacked my father and mother. So, they came to the camp in Kenya, where they still live. But

I don't know what happened to my three siblings. They fled the violence and we don't know where they are," he said.

Jean Claude, Dancila and their four children were resettled in Australia in November 2019. Since then, they have become part of the thriving Burundian community in Mildura, in Victoria's Sunraysia district. Jean Claude is involved with the local Burundian community church, delivering sermons with the support of the church pastor.

In Mildura, the family have been supported through Australia's refugee settlement program to obtain affordable long-term housing and complete an orientation program.

They are also improving their English and Jean Claude has been supported to access services and funding from the National Disability Insurance Scheme (NDIS). Jean Claude said the funding would help him achieve independence and support his family.

"I would like to be able to build my domestic and social skills so I can build my independence," he said. "I would also like support to enable me to increase my mobility to allow me to provide for my family."

He said that he was grateful to have a chance at a new life in Australia.

"Living in Mildura is good. My family is safe but I would like to bring my parents here to live because I worry about them. Also, my daughter in Burundi is vulnerable. She is being harassed and schools will not take her. I send her money but she is not being looked after. I would like to bring her here, but I'm not sure what to do."

Jean Claude said that with support from the NDIS, he hoped to overcome his disability and resume his career as a professional driver.

"Before the conflict in Burundi my life was good. I had a house and a car and I ran a transport business as a taxi driver and bus driver. I would like to get my driving licences and eventually set up a transport business here in Mildura."

CHAPTER 39
FILM EXPOSES THE HUMAN FACE OF REFUGEE JOURNEYS

A remarkable new film by Afghani photojournalist, filmmaker and former refugee Barat Ali Batoor chronicles a dramatic asylum seeker boat journey, laying bare the plight of people seeking safety everywhere.

The film *Batoor: A Refugee Journey* tells the story of Batoor's own attempted boat journey from Indonesia to Australia in 2012 as well as his longer journey fleeing death threats and danger in his homeland. It also highlights the plight of asylum seekers and the repression of ethnic minorities, including his own Hazara people.

Batoor accompanied a group of asylum seekers on a hazardous and ill-fated boat journey from a remote Indonesian island to Christmas Island in September 2012. On the trip the boat started to sink and Batoor and others swam to a nearby island where they were arrested by Indonesian police.

A still image taken by Batoor on the voyage won the 2013 Photo of the Year in the prestigious Nikon-Walkley Press Photography awards.

The seeds of the film were sown in 2015 when Batoor went back to Pakistan to document the stories of the Hazaras who were under constant targeted attacks and bomb blasts in Quetta City. The increased insecurity and marginalisation of the Hazaras forced many of them to leave Pakistan and seek asylum in a third country. Most of them tried to come to Australia by sea.

In his film, Batoor highlights the challenges the Hazara people faced effectively living in a ghetto; he documents their forced migration and the unseen and often perilous journeys taken with people smugglers attempting to reach Australia.

The film also takes viewers on Batoor's own gripping longer journey — one that reached a watershed when, in a photo series called "The Dancing Boys of Afghanistan", he documented the practice of "Bacha Bazi", a tradition found across Afghanistan involving the sexual exploitation of boys.

In the series, published in the *Washington Post* and *Stern Magazine*, he exposed a situation where young men are kidnapped and effectively forced into sexual slavery by Afghan warlords and tribal leaders. Because of these photos and his work with the western press, he was forced to flee Afghanistan.

Born in Pakistan, Batoor moved to Afghanistan to work as a photojournalist in 2005. His parents had fled the country in the early '70s because of the discrimination they experienced as Hazaras, an ethnic minority group in Afghanistan that has faced political, economic and social repression for more than a century.

"I just tried my best to show what is really happening. My hope is that the film will tell the story of people seeking safety," Batoor said of his film. "These journeys mix fear, boredom and extreme loneliness. They sometimes end happily, sometimes in despair and sometimes in death. I was lucky. I survived and I was quickly found to be a refugee and resettled in Melbourne."

In September 2012, he became part of his own story, fleeing Kabul with his camera in hand.

Travelling with 92 other passengers hidden below deck to escape detection by the Water Police, he shot a selection of images capturing the long route through Thailand, Malaysia, Indonesia and then by sea to Australia.

"It is a journey of sudden midnight departures, long road trips, surreptitious transactions, treks through jungles, and terror at sea," he said. "Few people — except for the refugees themselves — ever get to see this reality."

Batoor's boat ran aground on the rocks and his camera was ruined but remarkably, his images survived.

He was then detained and robbed by Indonesian authorities but escaped. Many of the other people he met on his arduous journey didn't survive.

He now works as a Program Co-ordinator with the Asylum Seeker Resource Centre in Melbourne.

"I'm pleased to have been able to show the real story behind these journeys — to show how people are risking their lives and enduring perils to escape persecution and the threat of death in their home countries," Batoor said. "I just tried my best to show what is really happening. My hope was that my pictures would tell that story. This is not about me, it is about my people and the genocide against them that is getting worse every day."

Batoor's family had fled Afghanistan forty years earlier because of persecution and set up home in Quetta, Pakistan, a city that hosts a large population of displaced Hazara.

He returned to Afghanistan in 2001 at just 18 years of age after he was hired by a photographer and a journalist working for British newspaper *The Sunday Telegraph* to be their interpreter.

It was the beginning of a journey that would change Batoor's life.

"When I went to Afghanistan and saw the destruction and devastation, I wanted to do something. Then I saw the foreign photojournalists working and realised that if I could also become a photographer, I might be able to help the country. I used the money I made as an interpreter to buy my first camera," Batoor said.

He returned again to Afghanistan in 2005 this time on his own terms as a photojournalist.

But the publication of the "Dancing Boys" story also brought death threats and in 2012 Batoor moved his family back to Quetta.

The situation in Pakistan was not much better, though. Other ethnic groups were boycotting Hazaras; they were being denied access to education, work and even the ability to walk to the local bazaar.

Batoor realised the only way he could support his mother, brothers and sisters was to find work in another country. He met with a people smuggler, paid his money and began a journey to Australia.

With himself part of the exodus, Batoor began documenting the displacement of his own Hazara people as they fled from Afghanistan and Pakistan to safety abroad.

The Hazara are a Persian-speaking Shia Muslim minority that is the third-largest ethnic group in Afghanistan. They have been persecuted in Afghanistan for centuries.

So, in September 2012, Batoor became part of the story, fleeing with his camera in hand. Travelling with 92 other passengers hidden below deck to escape detection by Indonesian water police, he shot a selection of images capturing the long route through Thailand, Malaysia, Indonesia and by sea to Australia.

The first night of the journey was calm, but by the second night the conditions at sea began to deteriorate.

"The water was very rough, and then the bilge pump stopped working. Those who were not seasick tried to remove the water in buckets, but more water was coming in than going out," Batoor said.

"Our boat was floating like a matchbox. There was screaming, shouting and crying. Everybody lost hope and we were thinking that this was the end and that everyone was dying."

Batoor's boat ran aground on the rocks and his camera was ruined but remarkably, his images survived. He was then detained and robbed by Indonesian authorities but escaped. Many of the other people he met on his arduous journey didn't survive.

"I am very lucky," he said. "Unlike most Hazaras, I was quickly found to be a refugee. I just kept taking photos; my hope is that, at the very least, these pictures can tell their story."

Shortly before getting on the boat to Christmas Island, Batoor had met with a Jakarta-based journalist from *The Global Mail* news website, Aubrey Belford.

Belford gave him his card and suggested they stay in touch.

On his return to Indonesia and with little money, no shoes and on the run, Batoor contacted Belford and they met at dawn on a Jakarta street. Belford realised the potential of Batoor's story and, more particularly, his photos and they were published that week in *The Global Mail*.

Soon after SBS aired a half-hour documentary on Batoor and other Hazara asylum seekers for the *Dateline* program giving the Australian public a close look at the circumstances of asylum seekers seeking safety.

Batoor's application to through the UNHCR for refugee status was expedited because of the media coverage he had received. He arrived in Australia in 2013.

CHAPTER 40
DARING ESCAPE FROM THE TALIBAN

Posing as a stationery salesman and wearing down at heel, provincial clothing, Afghan refugee Ahmed (not his real name to protect the safety of relatives still living under the brutal Taliban regime) made a daring escape into Pakistan under the noses of the Taliban.

As a senior Afghan government official, he faced prison or worse if he had been captured by the brutal fundamentalist regime which seized control of the capital Kabul on August 15, 2021.

After manipulating his social media accounts to throw the Taliban off his tail and hiding out with relatives for three months, Ahmed was desperate to find a way out for his family.

“I worked closely with the foreign embassies who were supporting the Afghan government. I was the representative of the Home Affairs Ministry in meeting with the embassies,” said Ahmed.

“We had US and Australian defence force advisors and it was my defence contacts in Australia who helped me get visas for my family. I had a very good life and a good job in Afghanistan and we had great support and advice on policy and operations; we were building our nation. But on August 15 something happened that was beyond belief. We didn’t think the Taliban could return but they did. The government collapsed. We knew the new regime was very cruel and would target those who with the previous government. Some people were taken out of their homes at night and their bodies were found on the roadside the next day. Many people in Afghanistan are now facing a tough life and difficulties. I was in danger otherwise I would not have left my country.”

As soon as the Afghan government of Ashraf Ghani fell, Ahmed went into hiding in a relative's house.

His first self-preservation response was to change the settings on his social media accounts.

"I changed my Facebook account to appear as though I was in Australia. I think this stopped people from searching for me and it might have saved my life," Ahmed said.

With eight children and a heavily pregnant wife, getting into the airport and on an evacuation flight was not an option. While in hiding in Kabul, Abdul's ninth child, a son called Wasim, was born.

After three months in hiding, Ahmed hatched a plan to take himself and his family beyond the deadly clutches of the Taliban.

"I was in hiding in Kabul until November 19th when I was able to get into Pakistan. DFAT had told me that if could get to the Australian High Commission in Islamabad, they would support me.

"I managed to get a visa for Pakistan and got to the border with my eldest son. The Taliban at the border checkpoint questioned me, asking where I was going. I had grown a beard and was dressed like a local.

"I told them I was a small businessman and was going to Pakistan to buy stationery and printers. At that point I feared I would be arrested which would have almost certainly meant I would be killed.

"I crossed the border and the Australian High Commission picked me up. The rest of my family were able to cross the border four days later on the 23rd November. The High Commission sent a vehicle to pick them up also — they were very supportive, beyond our expectations," he said.

After a few weeks in Pakistan, barely able to believe their good fortune, Ahmed and his family reached Darwin and quarantined for two weeks before arriving in Melbourne on December 12.

"We were greeted and supported on our arrival since coming here the local people have been very welcoming," Ahmed said.

Ahmed and his family are among around 3,000 Afghans to have arrived in Melbourne since the Taliban took Kabul amid dramatic scenes.

When they moved into a five-bedroom house in Tarneit, in Melbourne's west, they became the 500th Afghan family to be settled in their own home since the evacuees began arriving in September.

"The house is good and the neighbours are friendly and have welcomed us. We cannot believe the support and kindness we have received," Ahmed said. "We have received very good support from the start. One daughter starts school on Monday and two more of my daughters are starting English lessons." I have three sons who have finished high school, so we are looking at enrolling them in colleges.

"My priority is to settle my family. I want to get my kids into school and college because I want my kids to be assets to this country. Then I will look for a job. I want my kids to get a good education. Who knows, maybe one day they will help to rebuild Afghanistan.

"Before I joined the Afghan government, I worked for a foreign NGO working in Afghanistan as an HR manager. I've already sent my CV to my contacts in Australia. I don't want to just get money from Centrelink. I want to work and get some income. Centrelink is a wonderful initial support, but if you can work you should support yourself and your family."

He said his family feel safe in Australia and are looking forward to the future.

"We feel very safe here. In Afghanistan people face many dangers and restrictions and most parents are in fear that their kids will be kidnapped or come to harm. There are fundamentalists and different groups who are dangerous. We want to thank the Australian people and government. We have received great support starting from the High Commission Islamabad all the way to here in our own house."

Ahmed says he is worried about family still Afghanistan where his brothers, sisters and a stepmother remain.

And he is haunted by what happened in Afghanistan.

"The Taliban are saying that people working with the former government are spies. We were not, we were just trying to build our country with better systems and procedures," Ahmed said. "We were all working for the future of Afghanistan. But after 20 years and billions of dollars spent, we now have same regime that was so destructive before. And about 50,000 police were killed in the fight with the Taliban after 20 years.

"Now there is a huge humanitarian crisis in my country. People, including women and children, are starving and schools are closed. Girls have lost the human rights that were gained over 20 years. It makes me sad and angry."

CHAPTER 41
REFUGEE MECHANIC FIXES HIS FAMILY'S FUTURE

A refugee family forced apart by conflict and economic necessity is now reunited in Australia and building a new future together. To make a living Syrian refugee Habib Abdo Kammoush was forced to work overseas away from his family for 12 long years. He spent gruelling stints building roads in Nigeria and maintaining forestry equipment in the jungles of the Central African Republic. But when the war in his homeland closed in on his family Habib was forced to give up his job and take them to safety.

Now resettled in Melbourne, he has used the experience and knowledge he gained across the world to start his own heavy machinery repair business.

"I started the ATK Mobile Plant Mechanic business in January 2021 and it's going very well. I'm getting work all over Melbourne. I go out and repair equipment on site,' Habib said. "I work with heavy machinery, construction equipment, earthmovers and generators."

Habib almost has diesel fuel in his blood, growing up in a town where heavy machinery repair is a major industry.

"I started learning about mechanics when I was 12 years old working in the summer holidays in workshops in my hometown. The town, Maharada has many workshops that specialise in Caterpillar equipment," he said.

Habib worked in Syria between 1997 and 2006 when he moved to Lebanon to take up a job and then to Nigeria to work with an international road construction company.

Between 2016 and 2018, Habib worked in the Central Africa Republic with a forestry company shipping timber to Europe. Wanting to be closer to home, he then found work in Iraq, helping to rebuild infrastructure shattered by war.

"During this time the war in Syria was far away from my family," he said.

Habib would meet his wife Eve and young son Abdo in Lebanon every seven or eight months.

"We would spend 10 or 15 days together and then I would go back to Africa and Eve would go back to Syria," he said.

But as the conflict in Syria escalated Habib became more concerned for his family's safety.

"One day a bomb blast killed an entire family near to where my wife was living. I was not comfortable that my family was safe anymore so we took the decision to leave," he said.

Eve said the incident was a turning point also.

"It was very frightening. I had my young son with me when the bomb hit. I was worried about him and I knew it was time to go somewhere where my children could have a safe future," she said.

During the conflict, Maharada was targeted by the US-backed rebel group Jaysh al-Izza but remained under government control.

The attacks reached a peak during the course of the 2017 Hama offensive which saw suicide bombers detonate car bombs and open fighting between the Syrian army and rebels.

The rebels seized several nearby villages but were beaten. The family moved to the relative safety of Erbil, in northern Iraq, and applied for refugee status. They arrived in Australia in November 2021.

Since arriving, Habib and Eve have had a daughter Tia, now nine months.

"The first few months were very difficult for us. Everything was new and there is no one from our town living here. We have no family here, I have a brother in Nigeria and my parents are still in Syria," Habib said.

During the COVID-19 lockdowns Habib saw an opportunity to go into business. He was able to buy the tools, equipment and vehicle he needed cheaply as Covid-stricken businesses liquidated their assets.

He was supported by migrant and refugee settlement agency AMES Australia and refugee micro-financier Thrive in learning about running a business in Australia and gaining plant operating qualifications.

"I hope to grow my business and move forward so that my kids can have a better future. Here in Australia we have no fears about tomorrow. In my country you always have fears about what will happen in the future," Habib said. "This is a good place for my family. Things will be better for them when they grow up."

CHAPTER 42
REFUGEE ARTIST WITH PRACTICAL DREAMS

Having to flee violence and threats twice in her life has influenced the work that young Syrian artist Rama Kadrou produces. Her images convey an almost visceral sense of what it is to be a refugee and speak of the perils of refugee journeys but also of the hope and resilience refugees carry with them. And living precariously as a displaced refugee has also built a determination within Rama to turn her passion for art into a career.

"I think that because of what I have been through as a refugee, I can translate those feelings into my art and my drawing," she said. "For me, it's about describing visually what I've been through and also adding layers of feeling like sympathy and regret. But I'm also planning to transfer my painting to tattoo art. If you are working in oils or acrylics, it's very hard to make a living, it's more of a hobby. But I think I can turn art into a career through tattoos and I've started practising."

Rama and her mother and brother fled Syria eight years ago. She had been studying at high school in the city of Lattakia, on Syria's Mediterranean coast.

"But when war came, school stopped and I couldn't go any more," Rama said.

While there was no open warfare in Lattakia, the conflict meant a collapse of security in most of Syria.

"Our city wasn't that bad. There was no real fighting but it was still not safe. People were being kidnapped and ransomed. I couldn't go out on the street. So we moved to Egypt, but it was not safe for us there either."

In recent years Egypt has seen a rise in persecution and violence against

Christians. There have been attacks on churches and the kidnap of girls by Islamist extremists intent on forcing them to marry Muslims.

As Christians from Syria, Rama and her family felt under threat.

"It was really not safe for me to go out in Egypt ad I could not study or take courses," she said. "I basically stayed home for a year and half and practised my drawing."

When her family moved to Turkey, Rama was able to finish her high school education.

"I also studied at a small art studio in Turkey and prepared to take an exam that would allow me to study art at university," she said.

It was then, in 2015, that the family received visas to come to Australia as refugees.

"It was amazing to come to Australia, we finally felt safe. I've been studying graphic art but because of the Covid lockdown, I've had to stop. So, now I'm doing a business course online to help me start my own business in the future."

Rama has been drawing and painting for eight years and is preparing to study fine art at university. She credits her mother with stoking her passing for art.

"I didn't really know that I liked art but I started drawing. It was nothing really, just lines. But my mum saw something in it and she encouraged me to go a do an art course. I did and I haven't looked back. It's become my passion."

Since arriving in Melbourne, her work has been featured in two public exhibitions.

"I was part of an exhibition at a gallery in Sydney Road which featured five artists and I had another with friend who is also an artist," Rama said.

CHAPTER 43
PERSISTENCE PAYS OFF REFUGEE ENGINEER

Mustafa Ayobi arrived as a refugee from Afghanistan as an 18-year-old with no English, little formal education and knowing no one outside his immediate family.

After 12 long and difficult years of work and study, Mustafa fulfilled a life-long ambition when he started his first job as an electrical engineer.

He is working for Melbourne's Metro Trains designing and building electrical substations in what he calls his "dream job".

Mustafa arrived from Afghanistan with his family in 2008 fleeing his homeland's interminable conflicts. He had reached safety but a formidable journey lay ahead.

"I studied English at a language school and then I went to Minaret College in Springvale," Mustafa said. "I was 18 but in Year 10. I had language barriers and it was really hard. All of the other kids in the class were younger but were doing more advanced work than me."

After Year 10, Mustafa and his family moved to Perth where he completed Year 12 at Canning College. His family moved back to Melbourne after a year but Mustafa stayed to complete Year 12 and it was then that he met his wife Yalda.

"After Year 12 I was accepted into La Trobe University to study engineering," Mustafa said. "I was the first person in my family to go into higher education but now my younger brothers are following in my footsteps. I am proud to be a role model for them."

Mustafa faced challenges and barriers completing his degree; his friends and even his teachers tried to discourage him from following his dream.

"A lot of my friends told me to give up on school. They had jobs and new cars and tried to persuade me to join them and get factory work," he said. "And there were times when I was worn down and about to give up but luckily, I didn't."

Mustafa took six years to complete his degree, having to fit in part-time work to support his growing family; Mustafa and Yalda have two children — daughter Hafsah and son Habil.

"It was very hard juggling study with part time work and having kids but my dream was always to be an engineer," he said.

But even after Mustafa graduated things were no easier.

"After university, I spent 12 months looking for my first engineering job. It was devastating. Some of my friends even said, 'what was the point of all that study'."

Mustafa joined specialist refugee support and mentoring programs where he was guided though the steps he needed to take, gaining knowledge of the engineering sector, resume writing and interview techniques.

"This was really helpful to me in understanding what it takes to land a job," he said.

Mustafa works at West Sunshine, in Melbourne's west. He rises early each morning and makes the 50-kilometre journey from his home in Noble Park, in the city's south east. But he's happy to put in the miles.

"My dream was always to be an engineer and now I'm living it. Sometimes even I can't believe this has happened after all the difficulties I've faced," Mustafa said. "I came from a war-torn country and lots of stuff was always being destroyed. I wanted to become an engineer to help make things better and be part of the country's future development, especially in technological aspects. Coming to Australia and seeing how technologically advanced this country it is, inspired me more to chase that dream and become an engineer and contribute to Australia."

Mustafa's drive to give back also sees him volunteer at Monash Health.

He helps out with language translation and administration.

"I basically do anything that is needed. Now that I'm working it's harder to volunteer but I'm still available some weekends if needed. I want to be helpful and give back to community that has helped me and my family. And I want to help people who are going through what I went through," Mustafa said.

And he is keen to share his story among communities

"If I can inspire people through telling my story that would make me happy," he said.

When not working Mustafa is mostly ferrying his kids to swimming, basketball and soccer. As a young adult, he also had dreams of a sporting career in martial arts.

"But studying, working part-time and having kids made that impossible. But still, I wouldn't change anything. I am working as an engineer and that has always really been my dream."

CHAPTER 44
REFUGEE MEDICO RECLAIMS HIS CAREER

As a doctor working in Iraq during the conflict there, Asseel Yako saved hundreds of lives. His daily work was tending to battlefield wounds suffered by soldiers or militia members fighting ISIS or patching up women and children horrifically injured in explosions of gunfire.

Six years later he is still saving lives working a consultant physician, specialising in internal medicine at Warragul Hospital, in Gippsland, Victoria. The job is the culmination of four years of hard work, striving to get his qualifications recognised in Australia.

He had studied and worked as a doctor for almost twenty years before arriving in Australia but he was forced to jump through extraordinary hoops to be able practice medicine again.

The Occupational English Test he had to pass required a very high standard of English. Five small errors, include using the wrong tense when writing a verb, could have meant failure.

Asseel also faced an interview with the Australia College of Physicians after which he was approved to go ahead and find a job and then complete a medical traineeship.

He was lucky enough to secure a two-year traineeship at Warragul Hospital.

If he had not found the job, his approval would have lapsed after a year and he would have had to start all over again.

The interview cost him $6,000 which was not refundable if he did not pass.

Added to this is the $10,000 fee the Australian Medical Council charged to verify his qualifications and documents before he could even start the process.

Asseel is one of the few refugee doctors to gain recognition as a specialist in Australia although many have managed to become registered as GPs.

"It feels great. I want to thank everyone who has helped me along the way. It wasn't easy but it's been very rewarding. It's an awesome feeling," he said. "When I was trying to do this, many people told me I couldn't do it."

Back in 2014, for Asseel, in his hometown of Qaraqosh, even travelling to work at the city's hospital was perilous.

"It was dangerous simply getting to work. There were bombs, kidnappings and people were killed on the street. A friend of ours — a surgeon — just disappeared one day," he said.

Asseel loved his work as a doctor in Qaraqosh — a largely Assyrian city in northern Iraq.

"Inside the town things were dangerous but OK for a while. We had different people coming from other parts of Iraq to the hospital in the town. When the security forces were present, everything was fine but when they left after ISIS came it became ever dangerous," he said.

Asseel took his family away from Qaraqosh and eventually to Jordon in August 2014.

"My wife was pregnant and about to go into labour. We moved to Erbil — a ten-hour road trip — and after a week my wife gave birth to our son Darwin," he said.

The family stayed in Erbil until February 2015 when they moved to Jordan.

"We rented an apartment there and I worked as a volunteer in a refugee camp for Syrians and Iraqis because I was not allowed to work. We lived in a poor area in the town but even there rents were very high and life was difficult. After one year our visa application was accepted and we moved here to Australia. We arrived in February and lived at first in Werribee then we moved here to St Albans to be closer to some relatives who are helping us."

As members of a Christian minority in Iraq they were subject to repression.

"But things were quiet until 2014 when ISIS invaded Iraq — they are an aggressive and bloody militia," Asseel said. "We could not stay in our town because we knew they would kill us. We saw what happened to the Yazidis… they took the women, killed the men and enslaved the boys. In our town 100,000 people fled their homes."

Asseel studied medicine for five years and worked as a doctor for more than a decade.

"I am doctor. It is all I know. I saved a lot of lives in Iraq. It is what I was born to do. When we arrived in Australia we received a lot of help regarding our general life but not much support in terms of resuming my medical career. I still needed a lot of help in finding my pathway. It took about five years and a lot of money to get qualified and to pass the steps that meant I could work as a doctor."

Asseel says his family lived for two years as internally displaced persons (IDPs) in Iraq and received no support from anyone, including the Iraqi government.

"Since I arrived in Australia, we have received a lot of help," he said. "When we arrived my daughter Roxanne had pneumonia and was in hospital seriously ill for a week. In the aeroplane coming here there was someone who was obviously sick, he was coughing all the time. I think that is how Roxanne got sick."

Asseel said he was working hard to rebuild his life in Australia.

"I lost everything: my job, my house and the good life I was leading. I had just finished years of studying and now I have to start all over again," he said.

But Asseel is grateful that his family is safe.

South Sudanese singer Ajak Kwai has carved out a music career in Australia after fleeing her homeland. Through music she shares her own story and the rich culture of her Dinka people. For Ajak, singing and storytelling are central to maintaining a connection to her culture (chapter 15).

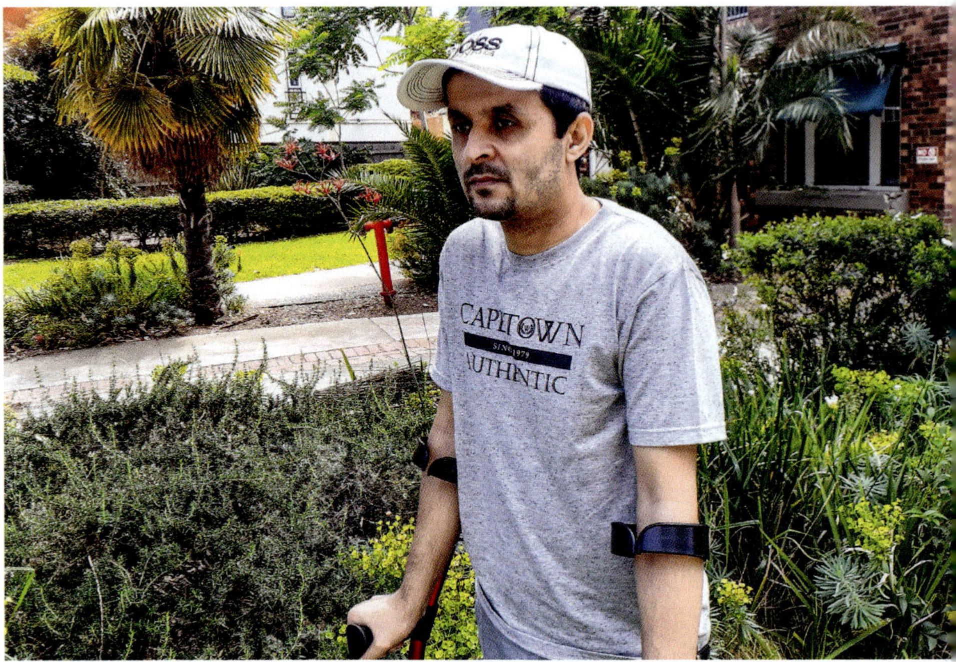

Afghan trauma surgeon Dr Abdullatif Stanikzai and his family were the victims of a series of violent terror attacks. He was shot three times; members of his family were murdered and he was finally forced to flee for his life. Now in Australia, he is trying to bring his surviving family members to safety (chapter 13).

In September 2021, the Afghan women's soccer team should have been competing in Asian Cup qualifiers taking on other national teams from Central Asia and the Middle East.
Instead, they were forced to flee their country after being threatened by the Taliban following the militant group's seizure of power in Kabul (chapter 11).

Four-year-old refugee Absaar Ahmad was at the centre of an incredible medical logistics operation. On arrival in Melbourne he was rushed to the city's Royal Children's Hospital where he underwent life-saving heart surgery for a rare condition that had been worsening in the weeks before he and his family were granted humanitarian visas (chapter 14).

As a doctor working in Iraq during the conflict there, Asseel Yako saved hundreds of lives. His daily work was tending to battlefield wounds suffered by soldiers or militia members fighting ISIS or patching up women and children horrifically injured in explosions of gunfire. Six years later he is still saving lives working a consultant physician, specialising in internal medicine at Warragul Hospital, in Gippsland, Victoria (chapter 44).

For Iraqi artist and refugee Bashar Yousif, paint and canvas is a form of storytelling. His work is informed by the trauma and displacement he has suffered at the hands of Islamic State and the other extremist groups that brought terror and death to his homeland (chapter 48).

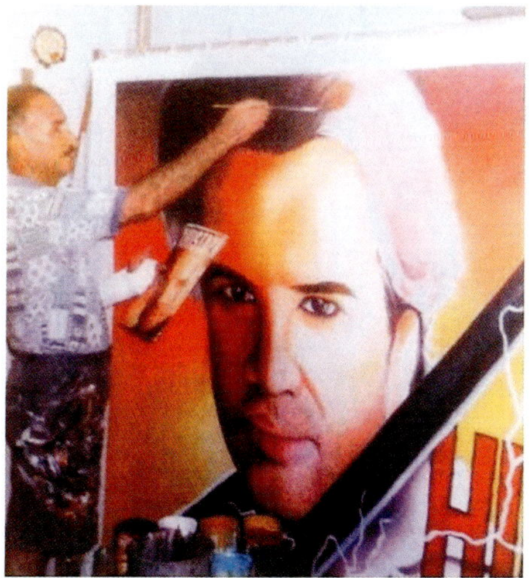

Iraqi refugee Zuhair Hanna worked as film poster artist for 50 years. Forced to flee their home when ISIS attacked their city, he and his sons are rebuilding their lives in Australia. Zuhair is now using his artistic talents to help decorate local churches and to document his new life in Australia (chapter 48).

When prominent Afghan journalist Khalid Amiri was desperately trying to find a way into Kabul's international airport to secure his family's escape from the Taliban, salvation came in the form of Australian federal government minister Senator Linda Reynolds (chapter 5).

Nelson Venturini's journey to Australia began on a day in 2009 when he was kidnapped by a criminal gang in his native Venezuela. Being threatened with a gun, forced to hand over his car and empty his bank account was the start of his journey across the world (chapter 10).

Unlike many of her compatriots, Maria Rodriguez survived the prisons of Chile's infamous dictator Augusto Pinochet. She brought her family to Australia in the 1970s where her life's work became nurturing her daughters and supporting them so succeed.

In 2014, the then Prime Minister Tony Abbott announced Australia would accept an extra 12,000 refugees from Syria and Iraq. The first to arrive, on December 17, 2015, were Iraqi Osama Butti and his family. More than six years on, the Buttis have become Australian citizens and Osama has voted in his first election (chapter 32).

When Celian Kidega fled South Sudan at just 17, he was setting off with his classmates on a long and hazardous journey on foot through jungle, war zones and across national borders. It was the start of an even longer journey that has seen him find a new home in Australia, raise a family and work to help others displaced by conflict and persecution (chapter 17).

As a 17-year-old Iranian refugee Ghanieh Daghagheleh made a dangerous boat journey seeking safety. Nine years later, as a nursing student, she was on the front lines of Australia's battle against the deadly COVID-19 pandemic (chapter 34).

Afghan refugee Jalal Ahmadzai is one of an entire generation of young people who dreams of a brighter future were swept away by the return of the Taliban. Despite having to flee his home, Jalal has hopes of returning one day to help rebuild his shattered country (chapter 26).

When a family of Afghan refugees moved into a quiet street in Glenroy, in Melbourne's north, they weren't expecting the welcome they got. Their neighbours – themselves mostly migrants or the children of migrants from across the globe – held a meeting to work out how they could help. Then they set to work (chapter 19).

Karen-Burmese refugee Kaw Doh Htoo was forced to flee his home three times. Chased out by the Burmese army who burned down his village, he spent almost a decade in a refugee camp in Thailand. Now, after rebuilding his life in Australia he has become a leader and inspiration to his community and has opened his own business, while also finding a slice of heaven in rural Victoria (chapter 9).

The settlement of Karen refugees at Nhill, in western Victoria, has revitalised the town by increasing the population and providing labour for local businesses. An impact study estimated the settlement program has added $105.5 million to the local economy over ten years, created an extra 156 jobs and boosted the population by 230. It also found that because of the youthful demographic profile of the Karen population, the Karen labour force will continue to grow over time, adding to the productive capacity of the region in years to come.

A group of independent Burmese journalists were forced to flee their homeland when the military junta seized control of the country in February 2021. They trekked through remote jungle and hills to find a sanctuary in Thailand from which to continue their work advocating for democracy and human rights (chapter 25).

From a small newsroom and studio in suburban Melbourne a group of exiled Burmese journalists are beaming news, interviews, information as well as hope and encouragement back to the people of their beleaguered homeland. The group are part of the Democratic Voice of Burma (DVB), an independent, not-for-profit media organisation that has been promoting democracy and human rights in Burma 30 years (chapter 25).

The small town of Nhill, in western Victoria, has become a haven for ethnic Karen refugees from Burma who have fled brutal repression in their homeland. More than 90 families have moved to the town attracted by job opportunities, housing, a welcoming community and a near-idyllic lifestyle (chapter 16).

For Bosnian-Australian artist Saidin Salkic surviving the horrors of Srebrenica have fuelled a cathartic and intense passion to create art. The filmmaker, poet, writer and visual artist says witnessing the worst mass killing in Europe since the end of World War II still lives with him (chapter 9).

Karen refugee women at Nhill, in western Victoria, have created a social enterprise called 'Paw Po', which means "little flower". The business makes colourful and artistic products that combine contemporary design and creativity with traditional, loom-woven fabrics. With a shop on Nhill's main street, the enterprise provides the opportunity for Karen and other women to develop and share skills, prepare for employment and connect with each other (chapter 16).

An influx of Refugee children into the town of Nhill, in western Victoria, has saved the local school and reinvigorated local sports clubs. The Karen refugees have found a new home and the local community has been enriched by exposure to another culture (chapter 16).

Tibetan refugees Palden and Tashi Tensing made perilous month-long treks over the highest mountains in the world to find new lives in peace and safety. On their separate journeys, they dodged trigger-happy Chinese soldiers, survived raging torrents and nights lost in dense forests; and they walked for days blinded by blizzards and half frozen by snowdrifts (chapter 3).

Refugee chef Rastegar Fathi was supported to start his own business by innovative micro-finance provider 'Thrive' which offers business loans to refugee and asylum seeker entrepreneurs who otherwise could not source finance. Rastegar's business 'Chubby Chef' Kebabs is thriving as a result (chapter 29).

Refugee photographer Elham Behin Hamgini has been able to start a business thanks to support from micro-finance provider 'Thrive'. More than 170 refugee businesses have received loans from 'Thrive' over the past two years (chapter 29).

Ukrainian women Ulyana Matsaienko has found refuge in Australia after her home city of Kharkiv was attacked by the Russian army. An apocalyptic morning punctuated by the sound of shelling and explosions marked the start of her perilous journey to safety (chapter 1).

A refugee family from strife-torn Ethiopia have found a new home in the quiet western Victorian community or Ararat. With the help local volunteer group Rural Australians for Refugees, the Wakjira brothers have found jobs, friends and a welcoming community.

Ukrainian sisters Yevheniia and Alexandra Cherkasova have found refuge in Australia after braving bombs and snipers in a desperate journey to safety. They fled besieged Kharkiv as Russian tanks attempted to encircle the city. After surviving bombing and missile strikes, the sisters were put aboard a train by their parents in the precarious hope they would reach safety (chapter 4).

The fabled ancient Syrian queen Zenobia, who fostered tolerance, art and scholarship, is the inspiration behind a new support group based in Melbourne's north that is helping newly arrived migrant and refugee women navigate their new lives in Australia.

"I want to thank the Australian Government for what it has done for us. At the time when we were in desperate need, no one else — except maybe Canada — was accepting us," he said. "I am looking forward to rebuilding my career in Australia and contributing to this country by working as a doctor."

CHAPTER 45
REFUGEE ENGINEER ON A PATHWAY TO SUCCESS DESPITE COVID SETBACKS

After being targeted by Islamic extremists in his homeland and forced into near slave labour as an exile living in Lebanon, Iraqi refugee Ramsin Moshi Butrus Kano is finally on pathway to relaunching his career as an engineer in Australia.

He is studying for a Master's Degree at RMIT after arriving in Australia last year. He had secured a job as an engineer but it disappeared with the advent of the COVID-19 pandemic.

"I was expecting to get a job but the COVID-19 crisis put that on hold," Ramsin said. "I was told there was no opportunity right now — not until after the pandemic and its economic fallout. I studied EAL (English as an additional language) at RMIT last February and finished the course. Then I applied to do a Master's Degree in Civil Engineering at RMIT University. I was accepted but I deferred it because I was expecting to get a job. Now, I have enrolled in a full time Masters course beginning this month."

Ramsin is an Assyrian Christian from a largely Christian town south of Baghdad called Al Dora. He studied a Bachelor of Engineering in Civil Engineering and had five years' experience working as an engineer in Baghdad.

Ramsin specialised in dams and water resources and began his career in 2009.

"My first job was working on the renovation of buildings and after that worked on bridges and then on a water plant for two and half years," he said.

But when Ramsin took a job as a project manager on some Christian church buildings in his town, he and his family became the target of Islamic extremists.

"It was difficult for us as Christians to work and live in Iraq. We were subject to a lot of discrimination," he said. "Because I was a Christian engineer, it was very difficult for me to deal with others and give them instructions for work. When I tried to do my job according to standards my life came under threat. Effectively, I was personally subjected to threats from a group of terrorists because I was a Deacon of the Syrian Church of the East and I was an engineer building church buildings. They threatened me, saying I should stop work and leave the country. They said they would take our homes and churches and destroy them. Also, the government in Iraq was not able to protect us and we were not able tell the government about the threats because it would get back to the terrorists and we would be killed.

"In Al Dora, the terrorists blew up many churches and killed people. The town was targeted because it was the site of Christian theological colleges. We suffered greatly; our homes and churches were destroyed in 2007 and '08. Things got gradually worse until the bad security situation obliged me to leave with my family in December 2014."

In 2015 their situation became so precarious that Ramsin and his family left for Lebanon.

"I travelled with all of my family to Beirut in Lebanon and we spent four-and-a-half very difficult years there," he said.

Ramsin was unable to work as an engineer and took a series of poorly paid, sweatshop labour jobs.

"In Lebanon we didn't have permission to work in civil engineering; in fact we had no legal permission to stay in Lebanon. I was forced to work in other fields. I worked for a flooring company laying vinyl and marquetry.

It was very tiring work. Sometimes we worked from early in the morning until midnight. I was paid $US400 per month but my rent was $US700 per month and I also had to pay for food and water. My father and brother were also working in similar jobs so, as a family, we were just able to make ends meet."

Ramsin studied in English at the American Centre for Language in Beirut when his family began to harbour the hope of coming to Australia.

"I learned a lot and it has proved to be very beneficial," he said.

Ramsin then went back to work packing food for a catering company. But he and thousands of other Iraqi and Syrian refugees lost their jobs when the Lebanese government banned refugees from working.

"Luckily just as I was sacked from this job in June 2019, our application to the United Nations to be resettled in Australia was approved," Ramsin said.

From there, things moved quickly.

"We had an interview at the Australian embassy in Beirut on June 19 in 2018 and on July 27 they called us to say everything was OK and our travel was arranged for September 12. My extended family all came to Australia too, my father and mother and brother and sister. We came together," he said.

Ramsin says he and his family are fortunate to be in Australia but there are many refugees — victims of the conflicts in Iraq and Syria — living in limbo with their lives and hopes deteriorating daily.

"There are many Iraqi and Syrian refugee families still living in Lebanon and they have been there for four, five, six years suffering the whole time," he said. "And after we left, the economic situation and the safety and security situation got worse. There are thousands of people suffering very much. They can't go back because it is not safe, there is no chance to travel somewhere else and no chance to work or study where they are — even children are not allowed to go to school. Thank God we left at a critical time — after that everything got much worse."

Ramsin's father-in-law is still living in Jordan as a refugee.

"They have been there three-and-a-half years. They can't go back to Iraq because they will be killed. And they can't live in Jordan much longer because of the economic situation — and the Covid crisis makes thing harder," he said. "Their application to join us in Australia has been rejected nine times. They are among hundreds of thousands of Christians in Jordan, Lebanon and Turkey living with littler hope, waiting to be resettled. Many are losing hope and their problems are growing. They face a dark future with no certainty what will happen to them."

But for Ramsin's family, arriving in Australia has brought relief.

"The first time in I arrived in Australia, I felt relaxed and safe. Australia is a great country and we are very grateful to be here," he said.

On his settlement journey in Australia, Ramsin has been supported by refugee settlement agency AMES Australia and particularly by case manager Balsam Hanna. Balsam helped guide Ramsin through the process of getting his qualifications recognised and through more English courses.

"She encouraged me and recommended to me what I should do on my pathway," Ramsin said.

Balsam said it was a pleasure to work with someone motivated to learn and study and improve their qualifications.

"We devised a plan for Ramsin and his family in terms of his professional career but also in terms of their health needs, schooling, accommodation, orientation and linking the family to the local church and community," she said.

However, Ramsin is determined to continue on his pathway and has started a Master's Degree in Civil Engineering at RMIT University.

CHAPTER 46
STORIES FROM AFGHAN EVACUEES

Between August 13–30, 2021, more than 120,000 Afghans were evacuated by military and civilian aircraft from Kabul's international airport following the Taliban's return to power.

Most faced retribution from the Taliban because they had worked with western governments or militaries, including Australia's.

In just 15 days in September 2021, around 4,000 of the evacuees arrived in Australia, more than 2,000 coming to Melbourne.

Names have been changed in the following stories to protect family members still in Afghanistan.

Saved by a phone charger — refugee family's electronic escape

A small hole in a fence, a kindly US marine and a borrowed phone charger were the difference between freedom and safety — and an uncertain and possibly grim fate — for Afghan refugee Nazari.

Nazari and his family were among thousands evacuated by military aircraft from Kabul International Airport between August 13–30, 2021. Led by the US, the operation also included the air forces of Australia, the UK, Germany, Canada, Korea, India and a host of European nations.

As a former translator for the Australian military and as a member of the Tajik ethnic minority, Nazari would have faced double dangers if he had remained in Afghanistan.

"I was working with the coalition forces as a translator and advisor — for the US and Australian air forces between 2011 and September 2020," he said. "My work was translating, advising and liaising with the local

Afghan army and people. I worked with the coalition across Afghanistan, my final place was Base Ochre in Kabul. After that I worked as a taxi driver. We all became very worried in 2019 when the Taliban began taking a lot of territory.

"When they arrived in Kabul it became even more worrying. After three days I decided we had to try to get out of the country so I applied for visas. At first I went to the airport myself — I thought it was too crowded for my wife and kids. I got into the airport and explained to the American marines that I had to get my family out too. They said, 'you have to get your family here'."

Nazari made a daring round trip out of the airport compound to try to get his wife and eight kids to safety.

"I brought my wife and kids to the airport. After spending days outside the airport trying to get it, eventually we got back into the airport. The marines helped us get through a small hole in the fence. It was very hard. We were there five days with dirty clothing and not much water or food. The sun was hot during the day and it was cold at night. But my phone had no power for two days and I could not access anything. But I managed to borrow a power charger and turned on my phone. It was then I saw my Australian visa. The US military people took us to the Australians who said, 'OK you are going to Australia'. The visa was issued while we were inside the airport and it meant that we could get on a plane out," he said.

After spending a few days at the Australian base in Dubai, Nazari and his family arrived in Brisbane on August 26 where they were in hotel quarantine for two weeks.

"We told the government people we wanted to go to Melbourne because I have friends who were interpreter colleagues already here," he said. "I'm very happy and excited to be here with my family. It's a beautiful place and it's safe for them. I'm not sure about the future but I will look for a job with the help of my friends."

Nazari said he was grateful for the opportunity to start a new life in Australia.

"We appreciate the Australian Government and people giving us this opportunity," he said. "We also appreciate support with food and clothing and accommodation. We are very happy to be here and we appreciate the help of Australian taxpayers."

But Nazari has fears for the future of his homeland.

"There is a dark future for Afghanistan. The economy is being destroyed and respect for human rights has been swept away. My family face challenges in the future. There is uncertainty but we are happy to be here because my kids have the chance of a bright future in this country."

Last man out — the plumber who closed up Australia's embassy in Kabul

Najaf was the last man to leave the Australian embassy in Kabul when it closed in late May this year.

As the building's plumber and handyman, it was his job to lock the doors after all of the diplomatic staff had departed. His role with the Australians put him on a hit list when the Taliban finally took control of the Afghan capital in August.

But the re-emergence of the Taliban and the loss of his job are not the first difficulties Najaf has faced or witnessed during his country's decades of interminable strife and conflict.

"I was the Australian embassy plumber in Kabul. It was a good job but in all of my 29 years of life in Afghanistan, I have never had many happy memories," Najaf said.

As a member of the Hazara ethic minority, Najaf and his family have always been potential targets for Sunni extremist groups in Afghanistan.

"Because of terrorist groups like the Taliban and Daesh carrying out attacks against us, I have lost family members," he said. "I have lost two uncles and a cousin, a maternal uncle, my father-in-law and mother-in-law. Two uncles went missing recently and were found a mass grave, Najaf said."

In 2017 Afghan police discovered a mass grave containing the bodies of at least 36 victims of a recent militant attack on a village in the Mazar-I-Sharif region.

"The last time the Taliban were in power in the 1990s my wife's parents disappeared. There has been no news of them to this day. My father-in-law was working with the government and their three daughters were orphaned. They were left with another uncle who was later injured in a suicide attack in 2017 — he had seven kids of his own," he said.

While grateful and relieved to be in Australia, Najaf said he was worried about family members still in Afghanistan.

"I am happy to be in Australia, at least my wife and kids are safe. But I am very worried about my extended family still in Kabul. I am from a village in Wardak province and there are Taliban who came from the same village. I worry they will look for my family. We are Hazaras, and Shia, and we are different from the Taliban — we are under constant attack from them," he said.

Najaf says he became a plumber at the Australian embassy nine years ago.

"I was the last one out of the embassy when it closed. I locked the door behind me. When it closed I went to work at the US embassy but only for six weeks before it closed too in June as the Taliban approached. At this point I was very worried the situation was bad and getting worse," he said.

Najaf's first application for a visa to come to Australia was rejected.

"I applied the first time and was rejected. But the deputy ambassador contacted the ministry and I got a visa," he said.

But it was then that Nasir's real challenges began in getting himself, his wife and two kids to safety.

"It was very surprising how quickly the Taliban took over Kabul. I stayed in my house for two days afraid to go out. There was a police station in my street which became a Taliban checkpoint. If they had found out who I was, I would have been taken away. One morning at 7am, I received an email telling us to come to the airport to be evacuated. But the situation was very bad. There was heavy gunfire which upset my kids and made them cry. People were throwing smoke grenades which injured my wife slightly. One of my brothers was working for TV channel and the Taliban came to his door. He had to flee and go into hiding. Only our uncles know his location," he said.

Najaf says he wants to qualify as a plumber in Australia and resume his career. But he says he will also work to get his endangered family members out of Afghanistan.

"We are grateful to Australia for giving us the chance of a new life here and my kids will benefit from all the opportunities here," he said. "But I fear for my family members and I want to help them to get out of Afghanistan."

First baby born to Afghan airlift refugees

An Afghan couple evacuated by air from Kabul in mid-August as the Taliban took control have had a baby born in Melbourne.

Shafiq and his wife Amira welcomed baby son Ibrahim on September 23, 2021.

The baby was born prematurely but safely at Melbourne's Royal Women's Hospital after the couple made a short 2am dash to the hospital from their temporary accommodation in the inner city.

"It was 2am and we went to the hospital in a taxi. Ibrahim was premature but everything was OK. The Royal Women's Hospital staff looked after us. We are very happy," Shafiq said.

He said getting out of Afghanistan was a frightening ordeal.

"It was very scary getting out of Kabul. My wife, who was eight months into her pregnancy fell into a drain outside the airport as were trying to get in," Shafiq said. "I worked on contracts for the Australian Government. I was a site engineer with a logistical company that worked on projects for the embassy — doing work on septic tanks and repairing sewage infrastructure. Because of this we were in danger and we were worried that if we stayed the Taliban would come for us.

"I had applied for a visa and when it came by email there was also a notification to come to the airport. We were told to go to the A/B gate. But it was very difficult. There were thousands of people trying to get in. It was very difficult for my wife, she fell into drain water. I was very worried about her. But we were actually lucky because it only took us six or seven hours to get in — for most people it was two, three or four days. We were also lucky because the Australian soldiers helped us and checked everything," Shafiq said.

Shafiq and Amira are among more than 120,000 people evacuated by military aircraft from Kabul International Airport between August 13 and 30 this year. Led by the US, the operation also included the air forces of the UK, Australia, Germany, Canada, Korea, India and a host of European nations.

The couple spent a night at the Australian camp at the airport in Kabul before being flown to Dubai, where they spent a week. After two weeks of hotel quarantine in Brisbane, they arrived in Melbourne on September 13.

"We heard that there was a strong Afghan community he Melbourne, so we decided to come here," Shafiq said.

He said his main worry now was family still in Afghanistan.

"We are very worried about our families. My father, mother and brother and sisters are still in Kabul. The situation there is very bad. There are no jobs and no security. We want our families to come here to Australia so they are safe. And they want to be with their grandson," he said.

Shafiq has a Master's Degree in water resources and environmental engineering from Kabul Polytechnic University and he plans to resume his career here in Australia.

"I would like to follow my career here in Australia. I will need to study because the education systems are different. But for now we are very happy to be here. We have had good support from the Australian Government. We have everything we need, including nappies and clothes for the baby," he said.

Shafiq said he was also happy about the opportunities Ibrahim would have in Australia.

"My son will be able to have a good education and follow his dreams while also contributing to Australian society," he said.

CHAPTER 47
ONE MAN'S MISSION TO HELP BURMESE PEOPLE

A refugee from Burma now living in Australia has launched a one-man campaign to raise awareness about the human rights crisis in his homeland that was triggered by the recent military coup.

Hector De Santos, who is in his 80s, has written to the Prime Minister as well as to 12 embassies of ASEAN and Asia-Pacific nations to protest the violence and authoritarian repression currently occurring in Myanmar.

He has also launched a Change.org campaign and written to the Victorian Council of Churches requesting they nominate a "Day of Prayer" for Myanmar.

"I'm trying to build awareness about what is happening in Burma. What the military junta is doing is terrible, it is inhuman," said Hector. "I'm just trying to do something, what little I can do to make a difference. I'm hoping that I can convince some regional government to intervene with the Burmese military."

In his letters to governments, he says: "With deep empathy for my fellow country people, I implore leaders of our world to exert pressure on the leaders of the Myanmar Tatmadaw Military coup for showing disregard and disrespect for the democratic wishes of the people and the duly elected NLD party and its leaders".

"I am not involving myself much into the politics of this diabolical debacle but rather want to highlight the humanitarian side of it.

"I also plead for the immediate release of Saw Aung San Suu Kyi and members of her party, the duly and legitimately elected party.

"Please apply all trade, military and aid sanctions immediately. Channel all humanitarian aid through the many NGOs in Myanmar if still in existence," Hector wrote.

As well as the Prime Minister and local MPs, the letters went to the embassies and high commissions of the US, UK, India, Thailand, Indonesia, The Philippines, Israel, Vietnam and Malaysia.

Burma has been plunged into violence after the military seized control of the government in February 2021, deposing the country's ruling party the National League for Democracy (NLD) after it won a national election.

Civil protests across the country have been brutally suppressed by the military resulting in hundreds of deaths.

Alarmingly, Hector says his contacts in Burma have alleged that the military is abducting protesting students from the streets.

"I'm told that young women are being grabbed off the street, sedated and raped and then dumped outside of towns and cities," he said.

Hector has first-hand experience of oppression at the hands of the Burmese military.

"I was a victim of the military although not is such a brutal way as is happening today," he said.

In 1962, the Burmese military staged their first coup and usurped the fledgling post-colonial democracy, heralding an era of Burmese nationalism and making Buddhism the state religion.

Under the *Burmese path to Socialism*, the army set about forming a Burmese identity, effectively marginalising religious and ethnic minorities in the country. For Hector and his family, it meant discrimination and the risk of poverty.

"They nationalised the economy and did a very bad job, so jobs were already hard to find," Hector said. "My Father was Portuguese and my mother was half-English, half-Indian. We didn't have the chance of having a future there, so we came to Australia."

As part of a marginalised minority in a failing authoritarian system,

Hector and his future wife, Wendy, had to assess their options.

Having met Australians through his involvement in the church, they instead aimed to move to Australia where the White Australia Policy was still in place.

"They didn't want to know your qualification, or your experience, just where your father was from," Hector recalled.

With the Burmese government censoring letters, the pair used a friend at the British embassy to smuggle their applications out.

"The British embassy was our only real postal service," Hector said. "After a long time, they told us I could come, and then once I was in Australia my fiancée would be able to come. I told them 'no', we must come together or I will not come."

Out of options and with pressure building, in 1966 they obtained a one-year travel visa and left for Thailand.

However, the Burmese government's isolationist policies meant they could not take with them any currency or objects of value.

"All we could bring was my wife's wedding ring, on her hand, and one of her necklaces, which I wore," Hector said.

After working for the US Navy in Thailand, Hector and Wendy came to Australia in 1969 as migrants.

"The people were very kind to us when we arrived here. Even though the government still believed in the White Australia Policy, the people were not thinking like this," Hector said.

Settling himself in Australia, Hector moved industry to work full-time in a food processing plant. A year later, he began to work part-time in restaurants during the evenings as well. Eventually, he added the role of wedding photographer during weekends.

"With my background, I could never become an executive, but I could almost make executive money by working two, three, four jobs," Hector said. "Was it hard? Not really, you just become very used to it. It was a lot though, we didn't sleep very much during that time. In Australia, especially then, there was so much work, if you wanted to work you could. So, I did."

Having retired from his three jobs to care for his wife and with his two children grown up and out of the home, Hector found himself at a loss after Wendy died.

"I thought, 'what could I do'? I teach English now. And I go to meet with Burmese refugees, to tell them about the free English lessons they can get. But sometimes they don't want to, they tell me 'no, we just want to settle', after everything they've been through. They don't want to go to a class, so I say that's fair enough, and just try teach them some basics and get them down to the shops or whatever. It's better to work, to contribute. I also help out with Friends of Frog Hollow. We plant the native trees around here, which gives the native birds somewhere to be, brings them back to the area."

As you enter Hector's house, you are greeted by a large white map of Australia tiled into the floor of the hallway.

"Yeah, I made that myself," he grins, "Australia welcomed me, now I welcome people to Australia every day."

CHAPTER 48
REFUGEE ARTISTS' PASSION SURVIVES WAR AND DISPLACEMENT

A pair of Iraqi refugee artists whose passion for their work was almost extinguished by decades of war are rekindling their lifetime love affair with art after settling in Melbourne.

Zuhair

Iraqi refugee Zuhair Hanna and his family were forced to flee their home when ISIS attacked their city but are now rebuilding their lives in Australia.

Now, Zuhair his sons Nawres and Yousif have settled in Melbourne's north and are adapting to life in Australia.

Zuhair, who was a film poster artist in Iraq for more than 50 years, is using his artistic talents to help decorate local churches and to document his new life in Australia.

A tradition in Iraq is to use art instead of photography in film posters. This has been the custom for as long as the industry has existed.

"It started for me as a hobby but I went on to work for newspapers and a cinemas in Iraq," Zuhair said. "My hobby became a career and I used to design film spreads for newspapers and write in specific Arabic fonts."

Zuhair says that before conflict came to Iraq, life was good.

"Before the wars came, people lived well and the economy was good. My passion was my art and I used to have an office with a studio. But we've had lots of wars starting in the 1980s and things declined. Cinemas closed because of the conflict. And after the war in 2003, things became more Islamic so there were very few cinemas."

With no cinema work, Zuhair took to painting murals in Christian and Orthodox churches in Baghdad.

Sons Yousif and Nawres are studying laboratory technology at RMIT University at are hoping to forge careers in medical science.

The Hannas arrived in Australia in December 2019 after spending four-and-a-half difficult years in Lebanon where Zuhair's wife and the boys' mother passed away.

They left their home in Baghdad because of fears over their safety.

"When ISIS attacked the city it became very dangerous especially for us as Christians," Yousif said. "When ISIS attacked, we had ISIS on one side and on the other, opposing them, were the Shia militias who wanted my brother Nawres to join them.. We left the day Nawres finished his university degree. At the time I had finished Year 11 but I had to leave school."

Zuhair and his family fled to Lebanon where they lived in difficult circumstances for four and a half years with no legal right to work or access to education.

"It was very difficult in Lebanon. We could not work legally, so we had to take any jobs we could." Yousif said. "I worked long hours operating playground machines and selling gifts but the pay was very low. Nawres did similar work and we earned only enough to survive."

Other members of Zuhair's family have been scattered across the globe because of the conflict, with a son in Sweden and daughters in the US and Canada.

The family has been supported by Australia's refugee settlement program and they have made great strides in their settlement journey.

"We are very happy to be in Australia. Life is very good here. We want to study hard and get jobs," Yousif said.

Bashir

For Iraqi artist and refugee Bashar Yousif, paint and canvas is a form of storytelling.

His work is informed by the trauma and displacement he has suffered at the hands of Islamic State and the other extremist groups that brought terror and death to his homeland.

"Most of my artwork has a message. It is very much influenced by my journey as a refugee. But also by my arrival in Australia and the opportunities that has offered my family," Bashar said.

"Each piece has a story," he says pointing to a triptych on his living room wall which shows the staging points of a refugee's journey. "The experience of war and being a refugee has definitely influenced my art."

One particularly poignant piece is slightly confusingly titled "Not for Sale". It reflects the horror of ISIS buying and selling Christian women.

Another piece is a mix of Arabic and Indigenous Australian motifs which Bashar says reflects his own real-life and artistic journey from fear and violence to safety.

"It also recognises all of the people in Australia and the government, all who have helped us so much," Bashar said.

Another canvas reflects Bashar's first experience of Anzac Day and yet another is a view of native trees growing beyond his back yard fence.

In Iraq, Bashar worked as an accountant but his passion was carving decorative images in stone which would then be used on building facades, stairways and walls.

Often, he would carve the Lord's Prayer using beautiful calligraphy. Since arriving in Australia, he has painted the words of the prayer on canvas in the ancient Arabic language of Kulfi.

Bashar and his family came to Australia in 2013 fleeing the war in Iraq. They were the target of threats from Islamic extremist groups in the city of Nineveh, in northern Iraq.

"They told us, 'If you don't obey what we say, we will kill you'. Before ISIS there were other groups trying to make Christians leave. Islamic extremists started bombing school buses," he said.

Forced to flee, the family took a 20-hour bus trip to relative safety in Turkey.

"We spent eight months in Turkey before we came to Australia. But we were lucky. There are other families who have been living in limbo in Turkey for four years," Bashar said.

"Things depend on the UN. I think because we had young kids, we were prioritised for resettlement. We are very happy and grateful to be in Australia".

The family arrived under the federal government's Humanitarian Settlement Program and settled in Melbourne's northern suburbs.

Since arriving in Australia, Bashar's work has featured in several exhibitions, including at the City of Whittlesea and Parade College and several have been purchased by the council and local businesses.

CHAPTER 49
REFUGEE PAYS A PRICE FOR FREEDOM

Iraqi refugee Alaa Rafo Alasguir was tortured by ISIS and lost the business and wealth he had built up with his own hands over 27 years to the brutal, fundamentalist militant group. He also almost lost his wife Rana during almost half a decade of life under the bloody reign of ISIS.

Since arriving in Australia in late 2019, Alaa and his family have started to rebuild their lives.

"Our life in the last couple of years in Iraq was terrible. There was blood and killing it was not safe for my kids and my family," he said.

Alaa was a wealthy man who owned two mechanical workshops in the northern city Mosul servicing large machinery. But because he and his family were Christians, the brutal militant group ISIS took away what had taken him almost three decades to build.

"ISIS hijacked our town and took everything from me and my family," Alaa said, speaking through an interpreter. "They constantly demanded money from me and they tortured me. Twice they tore out all my fingernails. It was a dark life."

Mosul, Iraq's second city, fell to ISIS in June 2014, with its leader Abu Bakr al-Baghdadi proclaiming the creation of a "caliphate" from its ancient and now destroyed Great Mosque of al-Nuri.

The insurgents hanged, burned, and crucified some Iraqi soldiers during their attack. Many people fled the city but those who stayed behind, like Alaa and his family, were forced to endure severe social, religious and civil restrictions. Very few children in the city attended school, unemployment rose dramatically and there were forced marriages, often of young girls, to ISIS fighters.

"I didn't feel safe. There was no freedom, no respect for any human being," Alaa said. "I wanted to leave I would have paid anything to leave."

The last straw came when ISIS thugs came to his home and attacked Alaa. His wife intervened and she was thrown against a wall, seriously injuring her spine and leaving her partially paralysed.

"When I took my wife to the hospital they refused to treat her. They said this was an Islamic territory and there was no help for Christians. This was not the Iraq or Mosul we were used to — the place where we grew up — where everyone was treated equally. This was the result of ISIS taking control of the city," he said.

The family moved east to the relative safety of Kurdistan. Alaa approached the Iraqi government for compensation for what his family had lost but his case fell on deaf ears.

With few options and what little money they had left running out, in January 2017, the family moved to Jordan in a bid to start the process of finding a new home somewhere else.

"But life was difficult for us in Jordan. It was very expensive," Alaa said.

The family spent the last of their savings — almost $US85,000 — just to survive. And Rana's physical health improved but her mental stated continued to deteriorate.

"There was no family for her and we were running out of money. We had our three kids with no schooling and future was very uncertain. Rana became very depressed," Alaa said.

Through a friend, Alaa learned about Australia's refugee program and began the process of applying for a humanitarian visa.

After two years and eight months living in limbo in Jordan, the family finally arrived in Australia. But it was not plain sailing for the new arrivals.

"I was very scared when I arrived in Australia. Our future seemed invisible and nothing was clear. I didn't know how we were going to live in place that was so different. A different city, a different language and culture we didn't understand. I was so scared," Alaa said.

He says the family's first month in Australia was terrifying. But he said the support provided by the Australian government and the refugee settlement program eased the family's fears.

"And coming to Australia has meant so much for my wife's health," he said.

Rana has received care for her condition after being referred to the National Disability Insurance Scheme (NDIS). She is now walking more easily, interacting with people and shopping for herself.

"Rana has made a huge improvement through the NDIS and the health service here. She has access to a physio, she has a specialist and she has had MRIs for the first time," Alaa said.

He said his family's ordeal has made them a stronger unit.

"We have been through a lot but we have been able to achieve some of our goals. Because of the support of we have received, I now feel my family has a future. And now I want to pay back the love this country has shown to us."

Alaa is volunteering to help newly arrived refugees from his homeland settle and navigate a new society as he has had to.

"I love this country and I want to help this nation be welcoming to everyone who comes here. I'm ready to help in any way I can," he said. "But whatever I do to help this country it will never be enough to pay back what it has done for me."

Alaa said his first priority was to help Rana to get as healthy as she can be and become more independent.

"But I have a big dream to get a truck driver's licence and to start working and then maybe to work as a mechanic again," he said.

Alaa says coming to Australia has also had a dramatically positive effect on his three children.

"Before, they stayed home and didn't feel safe going out. Now, they are more confident and are happy to go out. Each has different skills and each is working on individual plans for their futures. My daughter wants to be a doctor. And even though she has not had much schooling because of the conflict in Iraq, she has set out on that path."

He said that he feared for his father, mother and siblings still languishing in Kurdistan and would like to bring them here.

"To get visas, they need to go to Jordan but it is very risky and expensive. My parents are too old and my brothers and sisters do not have enough money. But still I will try to help them."

CHAPTER 50
AFGHAN REFUGEE CRISIS A CASE OF DEJA VU

When Kabul fell to the Taliban and thousands of Afghan evacuees began arriving in Melbourne, community leader and restauranteur Homaira Mershedi knew exactly what was needed. She marshalled friends and Afghan community members to support the refugees with donations of food and clothing. They also began raising money to support vulnerable people still in Afghanistan. Thousands of hot and culturally familiar meals as well as bread were delivered from her Afghan Gallery Restaurant in Melbourne's Fitzroy to the newly arrivals being housed in emergency accommodation.

Homaira and her group also collected bags of donated clothing and other necessities for the evacuees. Having fled Afghanistan herself during the Russian war in the 1980s, Homaira has first-hand knowledge of the refugee journey.

"The ability to help people has been really great for us and the whole community. During the first couple of days after the Taliban takeover a lot of us were extremely devastated," Homaira said.

"We have been catching up with each other on zoom every couple of days and supporting one another. For me it was Deja vu, everything that had been achieved in terms of democracy and human rights in Afghanistan over the last 20 years went back to zero. But it was pleasing and ray of hope that the Australian Government was able to rescue so many refugees. So, being able to support the people who arrived has kept us occupied and given us some hope.

"But it is still very, very sad about the situation on the ground in

Afghanistan and into the future that will be the focus of our efforts — the people on the ground in Afghanistan. We have to concentrate on those still there. We have already begun fundraising. We are open for takeaway on Saturdays and all the profits are going to Afghanistan. A lot of our customers have come and supported us, some have just come in and donated money. It's been fantastic."

Homaira came to Australia with her parents and two brothers in 1984 at the age of 12 following the Russian invasion of Afghanistan in 1979.

"Kabul under the Russians was very different for us, there were huge changes. I was very young but I remember being taught ballet by Russian teachers from five years of age," she said.

Homaira said that at the time the children of elite Afghan families were forcibly taken to Russia to be educated and indoctrinated with communism — under the orders of at the Afghanistan's Amin regime.

It was her brush with this policy that led to her family leaving the country.

"I remember one day at school being put in bus and told we were going on an excursion to the zoo," she said. "I knew my way around Kabul and I knew the way to the zoo and we were not going that way. We realised we were going to an airbase on the outskirts of the city. At that time a lot of kids were being effectively kidnapped and sent to Russia for education that was really a kind of brainwashing. But as we were going to the airport the bus we were in rolled down a small hill. Another truck pulled up, rescued us and took us back to school.

"At the time I was living with my grandparents. Both my parents had careers and were very committed to Afghanistan and its people. My father worked in the transport ministry and my mother was a midwife. My grandparents wanted to get us out of the country but my parents were committed to staying. But my grandparents took me to Pakistan without telling my parents and my brothers walked across the mountains to get out. They paid 40,000 in Afghan currency to bribe their way out.

"When we got to Peshawar they contacted my parents and said, 'we are in Pakistan, it's up to you what you do'. A month later my parents came and joined us in Pakistan," she said.

Homaira and her family were there for 18 months before being sponsored by her aunt and uncle to come to Australia.

Homaira's uncle Aziz Salehi had established an Afghan art gallery in Fitzroy in 1978. In 1982 her aunt Nauria turned it into a restaurant in to be able to sponsor and employ refugees from Afghanistan.

Art, antiques and tapestries embodying Afghan culture and history still decorate the two-storey venue, which hosts 200 people when fully booked.

The restaurant donates 80 per cent of its profits to Afghanistan, primarily through the Afghan Australian Development Organisation (AADO) projects focused on sustainable education and development of local communities.

After a career in medical science and also as an aid worker with the UN and IOM in Indonesia — working with Afghani refugees and asylum seekers, Homaira returned to Melbourne to run the restaurant.

"In 2019 I decided to come back to Melbourne to continue running the restaurant because of its great history and contribution. My aunt was getting tired and I did not want to see it close," Homaira said.

The restaurant, which provided sanctuary to Afghan refugees in the 1970s has again been pressed into service.

"It's been very fulfilling to be able to help. When the Taliban took over we were all in shock; all of my friends and family were affected badly," Homaira said. "For us, we had two options — to stand up and do something or just give up. So we decided we would help in any way we could. And it was beneficial for us to be able to do something.

"Since then we have received so many offers of support. It's been overwhelming, in a good way. I'm very happy to have been able to help and we plan to do more. It's kept us busy and it's been great to see the faces of the refugees and children we've been able to help.

"Since arriving, I have been active in the community. Australia is home now but I still care about Afghanistan and I believe there was a reason I was rescued from Afghanistan and that was to help other people.

"It's pleasing to see how this group of refugees is being looked after and we are very grateful. Twenty years ago when we had asylum seekers arriving with little support — we didn't have the programs in place that exist now."

CHAPTER 51

AFGHAN PHOTOJOURNALIST TELLS HOW HE BECAME THE STORY

For twenty years Omar Sobhani covered war and social transformation in Afghanistan as a photojournalist working for Reuters; recording the human cost of armed struggle as well as the hopes and dreams of a new generation.

He never dreamt that he would become a victim of the decades-long conflict that has beset his homeland. But in August last year, after the Taliban seized the capital, he was one of more than 100,000 people airlifted out of Kabul.

"We were evacuated by Reuters when the Taliban occupied Kabul. The city fell on August 15 and we left four or five days later by charter flight to Islamabad," Omar said.

As a photographer for a Western agency and often working alongside Western military forces, Omar became a target for the brutal fundamentalist Taliban militias.

"I covered war, conflict and daily life in Afghanistan for 20 years. I think I have watched the life of my country over two decades — across all the provinces. From the start of a new era of democracy and human rights and hope in my country — and then the end of that as the Taliban came back," Omar said.

Omar was caught up in a suicide attack on journalists in Afghanistan in 2018. Journalists covering an earlier bomb blast during the morning rush hour were standing in a loose group near the site of the explosion when the suicide bomber struck, killing seven people outright and wounding several, two of whom later died.

The bomber deliberately targeted journalists, presenting a press card to police before joining the group standing near the first blast site. Islamic State later claimed responsibility for the attack.

Omar was injured by shrapnel in his back and chest but his photo of the outrage was published on the front page of newspapers around the world.

He also covered an attempted suicide bomber attack on Afghan Vice President Abdul Rashid Dostum at Kabul airport in 2018 as he returned from exile in Turkey.

And in 2015, Omar covered bitter fighting between Afghan police and army and Taliban insurgents on the outskirts of Kunduz City.

But Omar's work did not always involve bloody conflict.

"Usually when we go to shoot for a story, we are faced with a bomb blast, a suicide attack, or some other type of violence here in Afghanistan. But I was pleasantly surprised when I visited Afghanistan's National Institute of Music in 2012. Even though I had lived in Kabul for many years, I had no clue this academy even existed — it was the only of its kind in the whole country. Foreigners and Afghans were teaching young Afghans how to play all sorts of instruments, as well as to sing. What struck me most is the opportunity given to women. There are not many opportunities for women in Afghanistan to play or sing music — during the Taliban era music was outright banned and women were basically taken away from public life," Omar said.

But in the chaotic days around the fall of Kabul, Omar and his colleagues were forced to give up their work recording the events unfolding in front of them to look after their families.

"Things were going from worse-to-worse day by day. On August 15 the Reuters office told us the Taliban were in the city," Omar said. "Our office was closed. It was in the same street as a lot of embassies — the British and

Canadian included. But the whole street was deserted.

“Everyone was trying to save themselves and their families. Reuters contacted the Pakistan embassy and they were able to get visas for all of the Reuters’ staff and families. Everyone was hiding in their houses or relatives houses. Twice we went to the airport in mini-buses. But there were thousands of people there and we couldn’t get in. We had wives and kids with us, some of whom were sick, so we decided we couldn’t stay at the airport. The third time we tried, Reuters managed to get us into the airport and on to a charter flight.”

While Omar, his wife and six children were flown out of Kabul when the city fell, his wife and three children were forced to return to Kabul because of problems with their documents.

“They had to wait for three months for a Pakistan visa. Eventually they were able to cross the border into Pakistan again and then come to Australia,” Omar said.

Omar and three of his children arrived in Australia in December 2021. His wife and three other kids arrived in February 2022.

“I can’t explain what it feels like to have them all here and safe after so many months. I’m very relieved,” he said.

Omar said he hoped life in Australia would deliver a bright future for his children and a new career for himself.

“We grateful to be here. My kids have the chance of a good education and a good life. I have a disabled son and I hope to get care for him. I hope to work in Australia. I’m not sure what I will do — I have no documents or equipment but I hope to continue my job as a photojournalist.”

CHAPTER 52
REFUGEES' BOOK TELLS OF AFGHANISTAN'S TRAGEDY

A recently arrived Afghan evacuee couple are writing a book on their experiences as the Taliban took control of the capital Kabul and they were forced to flee.

Civil engineer Fahim Farhang and his wife Bibi Sharifa began writing the book while in quarantine in Darwin after escaping to Pakistan in October 2021. Fahim says it is intended as a summary of the pain, suffering and challenges of the Afghan people.

"I felt I needed to do something while we were in quarantine, so I started to write this book. I aim to get it published to get a message across to people about what is happening in Afghanistan," Fahim said.

The book, with the working title of *Escape from Oppression and Terror*, also examines the impact of recent events in Afghanistan, including the flight of thousands of Afghanistan's best and brightest people.

Fahim says he hopes to draw attention to the problems the people of Afghanistan face and connect with the international community to make them aware of the looming humanitarian catastrophe in Afghanistan. He says that right up until the fall of Kabul to the Taliban, Afghanis had hopes of a peaceful and prosperous future.

"People were patient, they thought that one day the situation would change and they would have a comfortable life. For this reason, people were living a normal life and hoped with the intervention of the United States and the countries of the region, one day peace will be ensured in the country; freedom of expression would remain and women would have the right to choose, study and work." Fahim said.

Even with this hope and the Taliban at bay, life was precarious for most people.

"There were explosions, landmines, assassinations in all provinces, especially Kabul, where three to four landmine explosions occurred each day. Innocent and helpless people fell victim, Mosques were blown up, religious minorities were attacked, there were attacks on schools, and even to maternity hospitals," he said.

In his book Fahim tells of the fear and confusion as Kabul fell to the Taliban.

"There was the sound of gunfire. The sound of helicopters flying could be heard, I saw from the window of our apartment that flights were going from the US embassy and Wazir Akbar Khan area and everyone was fleeing to Kabul airport."

Fahim tells of his own family's bid to escape amid chaos and widespread fear. After several days of unsuccessfully trying to get into Kabul's airport and on a flight out of the country, Fahim and his family made a dash by car for the Pakistan border. They were stopped by the Taliban just 80 metres from the border where the Taliban ordered them into a mosque.

"We were all tired, exhausted, and upset, we were not sitting for a few moments when another Taliban came and told all the women to leave the mosque with their children," Fahim said.

Finally the family was allowed to board a train that seemed bound for Pakistan.

"We encountered Taliban obstacles but after spending half an hour in front of the gate in the cold weather with the children, we were allowed to enter the area and stand in the train with other people. At seven o'clock in the morning the border gate of Pakistan was opened and we started moving again with a crowd of people. The movement was very slow until ten o'clock. But then the train stopped and things become chaotic again as we located just two hundred meters distance from the entrance gate of Pakistan.

"Inevitably, despite the fact that my son and daughter were crying and scared, I sent my wife forward with the children and her mother because the number of women was small and they were able to enter for up to an hour. I watched from a distance as my son and my one-year-old daughter cried so loudly that despite their noises and crowds, their voices could be heard. I couldn't do anything, until they went to the gate and reached Pakistan. After two nights and two days, we were able to eat at a restaurant on the Torkham-Islamabad highway. It gave our children a new spirit in the knowledge that we were still alive and that everything would be fine and we would soon go to Australia."

Fahim was the operations director of Afghanistan's state-owned water supply and sewerage corporation and his wife Bibi Sharifa had worked with an Australian-led de-mining operation to make former battlefields safe.

Fahim completed most of his schooling with a backdrop of war as the son of a military officer. After completing his engineering studies, he worked with construction companies, the US Army Corps of Engineers Project, BORDA-Germany wastewater treatment and management projects; and with the Afghanistan Urban Water Supply and Sewerage Corporation.

Bibi Sharifa is a physics and public administration graduate who worked with Australian Army contractors and the Afghan ministries of education and finance.

Both are now rebuilding their lives in Australia. Fahim is studying a master's degree in engineering and Bibi Sharifa is volunteering at a local community while also looking for work.

CHAPTER 53
GLOBAL REFUGEE CRISIS — BY THE NUMBERS

The global refugee crisis has been called one of the great moral challenges of our time and if all of the displaced people in the world were a single nation, it would be larger than Britain or France.

The number of people fleeing conflicts across the globe has officially soared to more than 100 million people — more than one per cent of the world's total population — and the highest level ever recorded.

That figure, as of mid-2021, is up from 65.3 million in 2016, and 59.5 million in 2015, and amounts to 20 people being displaced every minute of the day.

The number has been driven higher recently by the estimated eight-to-ten million people fleeing the conflict in Ukraine.

Most (68 per cent) of these people have fled conflict or persecution in just five countries: Syria, Venezuela, Afghanistan, South Sudan and Myanmar.

Most have found temporary refuge in countries like Turkey, Colombia, Pakistan and Germany; nations that largely struggle to support the large numbers of people seeking safety.

Around 85 per cent of the world's refugees are hosted in developing nations and 35 per cent of displaced people are children.

According to the United Nations, there are about 26.6 million people deemed to be refugees, 48 million internally displaced people, 4.4 million asylum seekers and 4.3 million stateless people.

Also according to the UN, there are almost 2 million people in urgent need of resettlement. The number of resettlement places reached a 20 year high of 120,000 in 2016. Since then that has reversed with many fewer places available because of the COVID-19 pandemic.

So, 90 per cent of those in need of resettlement will never have the opportunity to make a new life somewhere else and will likely live out a large proportion of their lives in camps.

Australia is one of just 35 countries that welcome refugees permanently under the UNHCR program. The nation accepts around 14,000 refugees each year. By contrast, last year Japan accepted just 28.

Notwithstanding criticism of the way the nation treats asylum seekers, and especially those in offshore detention, Australia has one of the most generous and sophisticated refugee resettlement programs, taking in one refugee for every 1,400 Australians each year.

Since World War II, Australia has accepted 800,000 refugees from all over the planet. And about a third of those have settled in Melbourne.

Melbourne and Sydney especially have become a beacon to some refugee communities. For Afghan Hazaras living in limbo and without official status in Pakistan or Iran, Dandenong, in Melbourne's south east, is almost a promised land.

And for Burmese Karen refugees living in camps on the Thai border, Werribee, in Melbourne's west is a place where many of the countrymen have built new lives.

In Sydney, Auburn and Cabramatta have seen the settlement of large number of people from Indo-China and the Middle-East respectively.

A recent study shows that Australia's recent refugee arrivals between 2010–2017 were predominantly from Afghanistan, Iraq, Syria, Burma/Myanmar and Iran.

Meanwhile between 2001–2011, they came mostly from Sudan, Iraq, Afghanistan and Burma/Myanmar and refugees formed 12 per cent of all arrivals to Victoria in 2011.

In Melbourne, large populations of refugees live in the local government areas of Greater Dandenong, Hume, Casey, Brimbank and Wyndham and each area has people from a diverse range of countries with associated language needs.

In Sydney, the cities of Fairfield and Auburn are host to large numbers of refugees.

Refugee groups are attracted to areas with affordable housing with about two-thirds of refugee arrivals in 2011 in Victoria living in the 20 per cent most socio-disadvantaged areas in the state.

The other thing we know about refugees is that they are keen to fit in and contribute. Australia Bureau of Statistics data shows overwhelmingly that refugees and migrants are embracing life in Australia while attempting to adopt the nation's culture and traditions.

The snapshot of permanent migrants who have arrived in Australia this century reveals most of them work, are buying or own a home, have acquired high-level English language skills and become citizens.

The data, which looks at permanent migrants who arrived in Australia between January 1, 2000 and August 9, 2018 shows almost 60 per cent of migrants and third of humanitarian refugees owned or were buying house.

It reveals that 64 per cent of migrant and 78 per cent of refugees had become Australian citizens.

CHAPTER 54
CONFLICT, CHAOS AND COMMUNITY — AMES AUSTRALIA'S ROLE IN REFUGEE CRISES

The '50s, '60s and '70s

Since its inception in 1951, AMES Australia has played a central role in supporting the settlement of refugees who have fled wars and civil conflict across the globe.

Hundreds of thousands of displaced persons came to Australia as refugees after WWII. Many had fled the communist takeover of their homelands in the aftermath of the conflict. Others had not been able to return home because of closed borers or the fear of persecution. Most of these people left behind families or loved ones.

Almost all of those who arrived in Victoria received language tuition from AMES teachers in the 1950s and '60s in migrant hostels, language centres and workplaces.

In 1956 the Australian government struck an agreement with the Soviet Union and other nations under the soviet umbrella to allow family members left behind to come to Australia. Called "Operation Reunion", it saw more than 30,000 people from Bulgaria, Czechoslovakia, Hungary, Poland, Romania Yugoslavia and the Soviet Union reunited with their families.

The same year, Hungarians revolted against communist control prompting the Russians to send in Red Army tanks and soldiers. Hundreds of Hungarians died in the uprising and more than 30,000 fled to western European countries. About 14,000 of these came to Australia as refugees.

This scenario was repeated in 1968 when a more democratic government came to power in Czechoslovakia. Known as the "Prague Spring", the period saw reforms to the rights and freedoms of citizens.

But once again the Soviet Union invaded and removed the government. Violence broke out and again refugees streamed into Western Europe, many eventually finding their way to Australia.

In 1973 Chile's fledgling socialist government led by President Salvador Allende was overthrown in a military coup and replaced by the brutal regime of General Augusto Pinochet. Tens of thousands of Chileans fled their homeland, many coming to Australia. The exodus did not end until democracy was stored in 1990.

Once a prosperous and stable country in the eastern Mediterranean where Christians and Muslims had lived in harmony, Lebanon descended into civil war in 1975. The conflict lasted until the 1990s and left the nation in ruins. Large numbers of refuges came to Australia in the late 1970s.

In the wake of the Vietnam War, Australia accepted tens of thousands of refugee from Indo-China and particularly Vietnam. Following the fall of Saigon, the first wave of Vietnamese fled their homeland driven by hopes of achieving freedom, liberty and a better life for themselves and their families. The first wave came by boat. Following this, the then prime minister Malcolm Fraser allowed more than 50,000 Vietnamese to begin new lives in Australia. This was a courageous decision at the time as it came amid strident criticism, and one that has delivered benefit to the nation.

Vietnamese refugees who have made Australia their home are today making a remarkable contribution to this nation. Many of them started their Australian journeys at AMES Australia language centres in Footscray, St Albans and Springvale.

CHAPTER 55
CONFLICT, CHAOS AND COMMUNITY — AMES AUSTRALIA'S ROLE IN REFUGEE CRISES

The '80s, '90s and 2000s

Hundreds of thousands of displaced persons came to Australia as refugees in the 1980s, '90s and 2000s. Many had fled an increasing number of conflicts and genocides across the globe. Most were not able to return home because of closed borders, fear of persecution or continuing conflict.

Most of them left behind families or loved ones. Almost all of those who arrived in Victoria were supported by AMES Australia through language support and/or settlement services.

Afghanistan

There are more than 20,000 Afghans living in Australia. They began coming in the late 1970s as a result of the latest cycle of conflict in Afghanistan which started in 1978 when insurgent groups known collectively as the Mujahedeen fought a war against the Soviet Army and its puppet Afghan government. The conflict lasted throughout the 1980s in what was effectively a Cold War proxy war.

Between 560,000 and two million Afghans were killed and millions more fled the country as refugees mostly to Pakistan and Iran.

Since then there have been many internal conflicts between warring factions and tribes which saw the persecution and wholesale killing of several minority groups. Gradually the Taliban emerged as a dominant military and religious force in the country and the repression of minorities increases.

After the 9/11 terror attacks in 2001, the US and its allies increase their presence on the ground and ramp up air strikes with the collateral deaths of thousands of Afghans.

Over these years thousands of Afghans, particularly members of minority groups such as the Hazara, made their way to Australia as refugees and asylum seekers.

With Taliban's return to power in Afghanistan in August 2021, thousands more Afghan refugees have arrived in Australia, including many who worked with the Australian government or military.

In just 15 days in September 2021, more than 2,000 Afghans arrived in Melbourne needing accommodation, food, clothing and support to establish new lives.

The Australian government announced and extra 16,500 humanitarian visas over the four years from July 2022 to June 2026, increasing the number of visas for displaced Afghans to 31,500 over a five-year period.

The Balkans

Between 1991–2001 a series of separate by related ethnic conflicts, wars of independence and insurgencies were fought in the former Yugoslavia resulting in the break-up of the country. About 140,000 died as a result.

Most of the wars ended through peace accords, involving full international recognition of new states, but with a massive human cost and economic damage to the region.

The Yugoslav People's Army, largely controlled by Serbia, sought to stop secessionist movements and replace the dissolving communist system. As Slovenes, Croats, Kosovar Albanians, Bosnians, and Macedonians defected it effectively became a Serbian army intent of creating a "greater Serbia".

The conflicts were marked by war crimes, including genocide, ethnic cleansing and rape. The Bosnian genocide was the first European crime to be formally classified as genocidal in character since World War II. About 16,000 Bosnian refugees made their way to Australia.

In 1999, Australia initially refused to join NATO in accepting extra refugees from Kosovo crisis, offering only temporary asylum to visitors trapped in Australia by the Balkans war. This decision was quickly overruled by then prime minister John Howard who authorised nearly 4,000 Kosovar refugees' temporary visas to stay in Australia.

Somalia

Most of the 14,000 or so Somalis living in Australia are refugees who were accepted through Australia's Humanitarian Settlement Program. Almost all have arrived from a third country in the region, such as Kenya, Ethiopia, Djibouti, Egypt, Eritrea or North Sudan. They have usually spent many years, often over a decade, in these countries, living in refugee camps waiting to be processed. It is common for Somali refugees to be born in refugee camps in surrounding countries.

The Somali civil war is ongoing. It grew out of resistance to the ruling military junta in the early 1980s. After defeating the military government led by Siad Barre various armed factions began competing for influence in the power vacuum leading to fighting.

In 2000 there was a lull in fighting but in 2005, a sustained and destructive conflict took place in the south. Forces from neighbouring countries brought order over the next few years until the Federal Government of Somalia was established in August 2012, constituting the country's first permanent central government since the start of the civil war.

However International stakeholders and analysts still describe Somalia as a "fragile state".

Rwanda central Africa 1994

In April 1994 more than two million Rwandans fled to neighbouring countries of the Great Lakes region of Africa in the wake of the Rwandan genocide which saw up to 800,000 mostly ethnic Tutsis slaughtered.

The genocide had lasting and profound effects. In 1996, the Rwandan government launched an offensive into Zaire, now the Democratic Republic of Congo, targeting members of the former Hutu-dominated Rwandan government and many Hutu refugees.

From the mid-1990s, Australia has accepted several thousand victims if the Rwandan genocide and subsequent Great Lakes conflicts.

South Sudan 2011–2020

Of the roughly 3,500 South Sudanese refugees in Australia, the largest number, about 1,300, live in Victoria and most would have been part of AMES Australia Humanitarian Settlement Program (HSP).

Prominent South Sudanese in Australia include fashion models, Ajak Deng and Aweng Ade-Chuol, AFL footballers Majak Daw and Allir Allir, defence lawyer and New South Wales Australian of the Year for 2017 Deng Adut, Olympic runners Peter Bol and Joseph Deng, soccer player Awer Mobil, basketballer Thon Maker and lawyer and human rights advocate Nyadol Nyuon.

The South Sudanese Civil War was a multi-sided conflict that broke out in the newly independent nation between government and opposition forces. In December 2013, President Kir accused his former deputy Riek Marchar and ten others of attempting a coup. Machar denied the coup attempt and fled to lead the Sudan People's Liberation Movement in a war against the government.

Syria Iraq 2011

Around 100,000 Syrians and Iraqis have found refuge in Australia since the conflict there began in 2011.

The war in Syrian began as a reaction to the "Arab Spring" and grew out of discontent with the Syrian government, escalating into an armed conflict after protests calling for President Bashar al Assad's were suppressed.

The conflict saw various domestic and foreign forces that oppose both the Syrian government and each other. It was complicated by the rise of extremist Islamic group ISIS.

Venezuela 2014

Since Venezuela plunged into an economic and political crisis in 2014, more than five million people have fled the country. Thousands have come to Australia as refugees or migrants and many have passed through AMES Australia's settlement programs.

Venezuela has long been mired in corruption, military dictatorships and violent crime; and, since the 1980s, economic decline.

The most recent round of instability began in 1998 when Hugo Chavez was elected president amid disenchantment with established parties. He launched the "Bolivarian Revolution" that brought in a new constitution, socialist and populist economic and social policies funded by high oil prices, and increasingly vocal anti-US foreign policy.

In 2013, the inflation rate reached more than 50 per cent a year and the National Assembly gave President Maduro — who succeeded Chavez — emergency powers for a year prompting protests by opposition supporters.

Crime in Venezuela is endemic, with violent crimes such as murder and kidnapping often increasing annually. A UN report attributed crime to the poor political and economic environment in the country, which has the second highest murder rate in the world.

Myanmar 2016

For several decades, the Myanmar military has been engaged in the violent repression of the nation's ethnic minorities. And things have gotten worse since the military seized power again in the February 2022 coup.

The ethnic minority Karen have been persecuted by the Burmese government for 30 years. There are estimated 150,000 Karen living in refugee camps in or on the Thai border.

The Burmese army have systematically destroyed Karen villages and in operations described by human rights groups as ethnic cleansing.

More recently the Rohingya people have fallen victim to repression. More than 800,000 have fled to Bangladesh after the military launched a brutal offensive in 2016 against their communities in Rakhine state.

But the persecution of Rohingya Muslims in Myanmar dates back to the 1970s. Since then, the Rohingya people have been persecuted by the government and by nationalist Buddhists.

The Burmese military have been accused of ethnic cleansing by UN agencies and the International Criminal Court.

AMES Australia has supported large Karen and Chin communities in Melbourne's west and a growing Rohingya community in the city's south east.

Ukraine 2021

Ukrainians began arriving in Australia in February 2021 after the Russian invasion of the former Soviet bloc country.

Most arrived on tourists visas, which can be issued quickly but the Australian government said the Ukrainians would be transferred to humanitarian protection visas.

ABOUT THE AUTHOR

Laurie Nowell has been a journalist and writer for 25 years. He has written for publications in Australia, the United Kingdom and Canada. His work has been published in the *Herald Sun, The Age and The Australian in Australia and The Guardian, The Times and the Daily Mail* in the UK. Recently, working in media and public affairs for migrant and refugee settlement agency AMES Australia, he has been writing about the migrant and refugee sector while also working with emerging communities to help them engage with mainstream media. In previous roles, he was a senior editor at News Limited and an international correspondent for London's *Today* newspaper.

ABOUT AMES AUSTRALIA

From humble beginnings teaching English to new arrivals in makeshift classrooms in Nissen Huts in northern Victoria, AMES Australia has grown to be Australia's pre-eminent settlement agency, delivering services to over 50,000 clients a year.

Formally established in 1951, our organisation's antecedents were the hundreds of dedicated teachers who selflessly volunteered their time to help the thousands of new arrivals from post war Europe to successfully settle in Australia through the acquisition of English language skills.

Over the years we have continued to grow in numbers and expand our services.

We have been at the forefront of significant social change, supporting new arrivals as they begin to contribute economically and socially to our diverse communities. We have witnessed the birth of multiculturalism; a term that was new to us in the 1970s but which now we accept as an accurate description of the cultural and ethnic diversity of contemporary Australia.

In many ways, the story of AMES Australia is also the story of post war immigration and multiculturalism.

Since 1945 over 7 million people from 180 countries have migrated to Australia. 2016 census data revealed that nearly half (49 per cent) of Australians are born overseas or have one or both parents born overseas.

AMES Australia has played a significant role in successfully settling hundreds of thousands of new arrivals with our broad range of settlement, English language and employment services.

Our unique strengths-based approach to successful settlement, which recognises and harnesses the resilience of refugees and migrants and builds on their strengths, puts us in a great position to face the new challenges and environments that lie ahead.

We are proud of our history, our achievements and the continuing contributions we are making to our clients' lives and the broader Australian community.

www.ames.net.au